RECESSION-PROOF YOUR BUSINESS

LAWRENCE W. TULLER

BOB ADAMS, INC.
PUBLISHERS
Holbrook, Massachusetts

Other Books By The Author

The Battle-weary Executive: A Blueprint for New Beginnings

Getting Out: A Step-by-Step Guide to Selling a Business or Professional Practice

Buying In: A Complete Guide to Acquiring a Business or Professional Practice

Going Global: New Opportunities for Growing Companies to Compete in World Markets

When The Bank Says No! Creative Financing for Closely Held Companies

Tap The Hidden Wealth In Your Business: Use Your Closely Held Company to Increase Personal Cash, Maximize Retirement Income, Build Estate Assets . . . All Legally!

ISBN: 1-55850-024-3

Published by Bob Adams, Inc.
260 Center Street
Holbrook, Massachusetts 02343

Manufactured in the United States of America.

A   B   C   D   E   F   G   H   I   J

Dedication

To Barbara, Susan, and Charles

Acknowledgments

Without the encouragement of Mike Snell, this book would not have been started, much less finished. Thanks Mike.

A special appreciation goes to all my friends, business associates, clients, customers, and suppliers whose experiences form much of the foundation of this book.

Preface

Many of us get so caught up in the day-to-day turmoil of running our business that we lose sight of the basic principles of sound cash management. We all know these principles. If we didn't, we could not have stayed in business and achieved what we have. We all know that to prosper over the long haul we must keep costs under control, establish control of our markets, and exercise prudent caution when borrowing money.

At the same time, however, when business is booming, such as during the past ten years, we tend to ignore sound cash management principles. Blinded by the flash of success we cast prudence aside. We must have that new piece of equipment or that new computer or that new car. And why not? Sales keep going up, new customers come in the door, and banks are more than willing to lend us whatever money we want. Why not take advantage of good times? We have certainly earned a respite from the blood, sweat, and tears it took to get here.

Unfortunately, the story doesn't end there. Since the turn of the century, for every boom there has been a bust. Some more severe than others, but tough times nonetheless. Those of us who have survived tough times know how devastating it can be when markets dry up, costs skyrocket, and banks want their money back. It's never any fun to pay the piper for the good times.

Although the word *recession* appears in the title of this book, the tips and recommendations for sound cash management are applicable in boom times as well. In fact, history has shown that business owners who practice these principles consistently, not just when a cash crunch hits, are the same ones who lead the pack in growth and profitability. Prudent cash management in good times provides the reserves to carry a company through the tough times.

In 1991, we as a nation are facing tough times. Many industries don't feel it yet, but increasing global competition, a severe credit crunch, and the inability of our federal government to exert the pump-priming tactics used in the past to cure recessions, point to a continuing period of unsettled economic conditions. If your business is currently feeling this pinch, the tips and suggestion included in this book should ease the pain of recovery. If you are still enjoying the euphoria of booming markets, I encourage you to seriously look at these same tips and suggestions as prudent cash management ideas that should be implemented now, before times get worse.

A great philosopher once said that there is nothing new under the sun. It is true that sound cash management principles have been around for a long time. My recommendations for cost, sales, asset, and debt management techniques have all been used by other business owners to either recover from the brink of disaster or to improve an already profitable position. So I know they work.

Nothing is ever certain in this world. But the odds are very high that ignoring the signs of an oncoming cash crunch most certainly will cause harm to all of us. Take heed and Godspeed!

—*Lawrence W. Tuller*

Table Of Contents

Chapter 4

Chapter 5

Chapter 6

Chapter 7

Chapter 8

Chapter 9

Chapter 10

Chapter 11

Chapter 12

Chapter 1

Getting It All Together

Developing Strategies to Increase Cash

Tough times demand tough actions. Friends and competitors close their doors for the final time. Bankruptcy courts fill to overflowing. You could be next, unless you take dramatic actions to recession-proof your business: not tomorrow, not next week, but right now!

Shakeouts in banking institutions, real-estate developers, construction companies, and aerospace contractors foreshadow dropping sales and skyrocketing costs in many other industries. Federal fiscal mismanagement, a drying up of business credit, strengthening foreign competition, increasing inflation and un-employment rates, reduced capital formation, and a pulling back of consumer spending, can only mean tough times ahead. Will this turmoil last for six months, a year, two years, more? No one knows. Economists from every think tank in the nation have different views.

From the viewpoint of business owners, it really doesn't make much difference. Whenever the current recession ends, competitive advantage, business structures, employee objectives, and technology will certainly have changed from last year, or even last month. If you are going to survive tough times, specific actions must be implemented to take advantage of these changing conditions.

A company must enter these new economic times tougher and leaner than it ever was in the past. It must exploit the financial, personnel, and market resources at its disposal in the most efficient ways possible. It must aggressively attack competition. It must slice out bureaucratic fat and change unproductive policies.

One cardinal rule stands out as the primary requirement for surviving in tough times: the amount of cash available for discretionary use must be increased beyond normal operating levels. The reason is obvious. As competition forces sales down, the amount of cash coming in drops. As inflation drives material and labor costs up, more cash goes out the door. Fixed occupancy costs must be paid regardless of how much sales are generated. And finally, principal and interest payments on bank debt must be met without consideration for the level of cash available from operations.

The big question facing every business owner is, "How do I increase cash flow beyond normal operating levels without jeopardizing the future of my business?"

Answering this crucial question is what this book is all about.

The succeeding chapters present a variety of cash-generating methods. They have all been used successfully by other business owners to turn the tables on tough times. All of these ideas won't be applicable to all businesses. Some can be used only by manufacturing companies. Others uniquely fit service companies. Market definition, location, and company size influence which steps will help you. And whether you are already experiencing tough times or anticipating future problems determines the speed with which some of these recommendations must be implemented.

Most of the suggestions, however, are universally applicable to some degree. The book has been structured to encourage the choice of only those topics within each chapter that can help in your specific situation.

In virtually any business, regardless of size or industry, cash flow can be increased by four methods.

1. Decreasing costs
2. Increasing sales

3. Selling assets

4. Reducing debt payments

At first glance, it might appear that during tough times none of these steps is practical. How can you cut costs when material increases average nearly 2 percent per month and wages and benefits are going up 5 to 10 percent per year? How can you increase sales in a shrinking market with decreasing prices? How can you sell assets when you need everything either now or in the future? And how can you reduce bank debt without paying out additional cash?

Tough questions. But then, these are tough times.

Increasing Cash Flow through Cost Reductions

Any business, large or small, manufacturing, distribution, service, or retail, has the capability of reducing at least some operating costs. A common rule of thumb is that any business, of any size, in any industry, can always reduce costs by at least 10 percent. But it takes courage. And it takes determination.

A close look at employee costs is usually a good place to start. Can you get by with fewer production people? By trimming product lines fewer workers should be required. How about personnel in sales, order taking, customer service, order expediting, shipping and receiving? With realigned marketing strategies at least some of these people could be let go.

Excessive administrative overhead is a luxury few companies can afford during tough times. Can you hire an outside bookkeeper or accounting firm at less cost than doing the work in-house? The preparation of payroll, sales, use, property, income and other tax returns can easily be done on the outside. So can financial statements and bank reports.

Contracting on the outside for data-processing services, janitorial work, deliveries to and from the plant, and building and equipment maintenance is nearly always less expensive than having employees do the work.

Do you really need all those managers and supervisors? How about subcontracting personnel work—employee benefits, pension administration, and worker's compensation compliance? Replacing employees with family members may not generate extra cash—or maybe it will. As a minimum, however, more cash stays at home. Company cars may be a convenience when times are good, but now, how about subleasing them to employees to increase cash flow? Or doing away with them completely?

Reducing costs is an absolute necessity to recession-proof a company. There are always some costs that can be eliminated or curtailed. Every cost dollar saved increases much needed cash flow. Chapter 2 lays out methods for reducing manufactured product costs. It also describes how to construct a formal cost-reduction program and then how to monitor the program to be sure of getting the reductions you plan. Practical, short-term actions to reduce personnel costs are identified in chapter 3. Hard-hitting ideas for reducing administrative and selling costs can be found in chapters 4 through 7. Practical recommendations for reducing debt service payments are found in chapter 9.

Increasing Cash Flow through Sales

Several tactics can be used to increase cash flow in the sales area. By pruning low-margin or low-volume products or services you can redirect limited resources to fewer but more profitable lines and customers. Special pricing incentives invite customers to buy higher profit items as well as promotional goods. Capturing new market niches multiplies the customer base.

Advertising campaigns that pinpoint specific products or services attract new markets or customers. A public relations program that puts your company name on the map can also bring in additional business. Shifting a market mix may stimulate sales of previously dormant items.

Sales promotion programs might actually allow you to raise prices on some items. Payment discounts and improved collection procedures move cash into the business faster. Incentive policies for customer returns coupled with same-day deliveries might stimulate a faster sales turnover. Special discounts in conjunction with COD terms for customer pickups inevitably improves turnover and speeds cash flow. Perhaps an in-house training program for customer personnel would improve your customer service image.

Changing from a salaried to a commission sales force saves cash by matching personnel costs with sales. Direct selling efforts by you and other management personnel often improves customer service and garners new orders. By redirecting other selling costs to productive channels you can gain substantial savings and increased selling productivity. Cooperative sales incentives and advertising campaigns with large customers, and even competitors, is another avenue for reducing selling expenses.

A myriad of possibilities exist for generating additional cash through sales channels—even during tough times. Frequently, all it takes is a little creative initiative on your part. In other cases, small cash investments yield substantial new sales. Chapters 5, 6, and 7, define these and other marketing alternatives for increasing cash flow through sales. Chapter 11 presents practical suggestions for saving your business if markets begin deteriorating.

Increasing Cash by Selling Assets

Nearly every company needs assets of one type or another. Some use production equipment and machinery. Others require office equipment: computers, typewriters, printers. Office furniture and fixtures are common to all companies. Many businesses own vehicles: cars, trucks, and forklifts. Perhaps you made a quick killing in the past and invested in an airplane, a yacht, or a lodge for customer entertaining. Manufacturing, retail, and distribution companies keep inventory. All businesses utilize office, warehouse, production, or sales space of some type.

In addition to reducing costs and increasing profitable sales, a third way to raise additional cash is to sell assets that are not crucial to survival. For many companies this seems to be the most difficult move to make.

It's human nature to feel that even if we don't use that extra desk or delivery truck right now, we might have a need for it in the future. We also enjoy the luxury of being comfortable with what we have and where we are.

But tough times demand a close look at what is really needed, right now, and disposing of the balance—for cash.

Chapter 8 gives hard-core suggestions for disposing of machinery, equipment, furniture and fixtures, vehicles, materials, and supplies that are not essential to today's survival. It also recommends how to get the best prices.

Unused building space in a production facility, office, warehouse, or store can usually be leased out to generate cash. And why not? It may be convenient to have extra storage space, a file room, lunch tables, or meeting rooms, but such luxuries don't pay the bills. When recession-proofing, it's cash that counts, not conveniences. Methods for accomplishing this are also included in chapter 8.

Some business owners go to the extreme. They subcontract administrative functions, move their office to their home, and lease out the entire office. Such a person is Robert Turnblood, the owner of a local advertising agency.

When business was booming, Robert's agency turned annual sales of over $3 million. As clients began skimping on their advertising programs, Robert saw that his office and staff were just too much overhead to carry. He talked his CPA into doing the bookkeeping chores, hired an independent contractor to prepare client billings from home, moved his office furniture into a spare room in his house, and leased out the entire 4,000 square feet of office space previously occupied by his agency.

The added cash was enough to tide him over for three years, at which time new clients were added. Rather than reopening another office, Robert merely added an extra room to his house, hired a part-time secretary, and continued subcontracting the rest of the jobs. He is still operating this way today and his annual billings have doubled.

Increasing Cash by Reducing Debt Service

Some companies are fortunate not to have succumbed to the temptations of bank loans. Most of us, however, could not expand our businesses without bank debt. As long as our businesses grow, everyone benefits. The bank makes money, the company leverages its growth, and increasing sales generate enough cash to meet the debt service payments. In a downturn, however, debt service payments can easily sink an otherwise salvageable business, as the alarming increase in bankruptcies proves.

Companies that have borrowed heavily against inventory and receivables face a real problem in a business downturn. When inventory and receivables are increasing, a revolving line of credit brings cash into the business faster than normal. But in a downturn, with inventory and receivables decreasing the reverse occurs: the amount paid back to the bank each month frequently exceeds new purchases and orders shipped. Excess cash from sales, which is normally used for operating expenses, now must be returned to the bank.

Businesses saddled with fixed debt payments or a revolving line of credit can free up an enormous amount of cash if a way can be found to reduce or eliminate this outpouring to banks. This is never an easy task. In tough times it's even more difficult with banks becoming more obstreperous, credit drying up, and increasing loan defaults alerting lenders to be especially watchful for potential delinquencies.

Several possibilities exist, however. Given the right circumstances, exchanging part of the debt for company stock works wonders. In other cases, it's possible to convert a revolver into a term loan. Converting short-term loans into longer-term obligations is a good solution if unsecured assets can be pledged. Refinancing under more favorable terms with another bank often helps.

All of these methods and several others are described in detail in chapters 9 and 12. Regardless of the method used, restructuring a company's debt to increase liquidity always adds to the amount of cash available for operating needs.

Some small businesses face another financing hurdle during tough times. Cyclical or seasonal businesses and those with customer dating programs need to get short-term loans to carry them through the dry spells. With bank credit drying up, cash from other sources must be found. Business owners with this problem can also fine helpful ideas in chapter 9.

Preparing a Cash-Flow Plan

It always helps to have the right tools to change a tire or repair a leaky faucet. The same holds true in recession-proofing a company. The two basic tools for this task are a cash-flow plan and a cost-reduction plan.

I know that some entrepreneurs turn red whenever they hear the word *plan*. Every business book they pick up pushes plans. Bankers insist on a repayment plan before granting loans. They are sick and tired of people telling them they must have a plan to run their business profitably when over the years they have made a fortune without any plan at all.

In tough times, when every dollar counts, it seems to me that using planning tools is a small price to pay for survival. For over thirty years I have worked with business owners and managers to save their companies and divisions. In hundreds of instances, I have never seen a company survive tough times without using both a cash-flow plan and a cost-reduction plan.

There must be some tool to organize actions and to monitor the success or failure of these actions. Any business, large or small, is too complex and dynamic to mentally keep track of every action taken to improve cash flow. Six months from now, when extemporaneous recession-proofing actions fail and the company dies, it's too late to change direction. With a cash-flow plan and a cost-reduction plan you can see where you are heading and take corrective actions before it's too late.

A cash-flow plan is a detailed, written document that identifies what cash flow can be expected by month for at least twelve months out. Companies with longer production or sales cycles find a two- or three-year projection helpful.

A cash-flow plan is a working tool. It is an action plan, alive, dynamic, changeable. It will be used continuously as the basis for tactical actions. It acts as a monitoring device to be certain that operating strategies you want to be followed actually are being followed. It is as different from the garden variety business plan as night is from day.

A well-constructed cash-flow plan provides a road map for everyone in the organization. It lays out in legible terms the cash coming in and the cash going out from every business action: from increasing an advertising program to laying off three employees, from leasing out space to selling a piece of equipment to implementing a sales promotion. Even more important, a cash-flow plan specifically identifies where and when you will be short of cash. If carefully prepared it gives you advance warning of danger signals on the horizon so you can change course.

You don't have to be an accountant or a bookkeeper to construct a cash-flow plan. In fact, such background often confuses the issue. A cash-flow plan has little resemblance to traditional financial statements—balance sheets and income statements. It deals only in the cash result of business actions—how much cash comes in, how much cash goes out, and when these conditions are expected to happen.

If you are uncomfortable working with numbers, hire someone on a part-time basis to help, perhaps a public accountant or a retired bookkeeper. They won't charge that much, and it can save a lot of your valuable time. It usually doesn't work very well to have anyone on your payroll do the calculations. Employees have their own agendas for keeping their jobs and this invariably distorts the results of the plan.

A cash-flow plan is strictly an internal document. It won't be handed to bankers, employees, suppliers, or the IRS. It doesn't need to be bound in a fancy booklet. It can be done on a personal computer, a columnar tablet, or the back of a grocery bag. It certainly doesn't need to be typed. It's for you to use as a management tool for recession-proofing your business.

A cash-flow plan consists of four sections.

1. A cost-reduction program

2. Marketing and sales strategies

3. An asset disposal plan

4. A debt-reduction plan

Succeeding chapters present ideas and recommendations to generate cash flow in each of these areas. To put it all together, however, a summary schedule is useful. The total cash receipts and cash expenditures expected from actions in each of these operating activities is transferred to a format that can be easily used for monitoring daily, weekly, and monthly cash flow.

I won't bore you with forms. You can't use those appearing in books anyway unless you tear the book apart. And then the form will be the wrong size or have the wrong headings. It doesn't make any difference what the format is as long as it makes sense to you.

One important matter to remember, however, is that the cash-flow plan should be structured to record expected cash coming in from all sources and cash going out for all types of payments. It should be divided into small enough increments to be able to monitor actual results against it (preferably monthly, in some cases weekly).

Very small companies or those selling only one or two product lines can get by with a very simple cash-flow plan. If you have two employees and plan to lay off one, it's a snap to know how much cash you'll save and you sure don't need a form to tell you. If you plan to sell that old printing press next month, once you get a bid price, you know exactly how much extra cash you'll have. And clearly, if you are the only employee you can figure out in five minutes what costs you can cut.

If the shoe fits, skip the rest of this chapter because it applies to slightly larger companies. Go on to the following chapters for some hard-core cash generating ideas that should help get you going in the right direction.

Companies with ten, twenty, thirty, or more employees or several product lines or multiple locations must of necessity construct a more formal and detailed cash-flow plan.

For example, if you have thirty employees, some hourly, some salaried, with a variety of wage rates and benefit programs, preparing a detailed payroll forecast is practically a necessity. You would have to be a mathematical genius to do all the calculations in your head. You need to calculate hours worked, payroll taxes, group insurance, contributions to SEP or 401(k) retirement plans, worker's compensation, vacations, and holidays.

When you finish this payroll forecast, slip the totals by month into the cash-flow plan summary. You will probably also want to record the current payroll details as the starting point for a cost-reduction plan. Future employee terminations are then projected as part of this plan. Detailed payroll schedules are also used in preparing operating budgets to monitor the results of cost reductions as seen in the following chapter.

Cash Receipts

A separate sheet should be used to project anticipated cash receipts. The layout is irrelevant as long as it provides space for detailed cash receipt projections.

The cash receipts section projects all incoming cash from every source.

- ☐ Collections from receivables
- ☐ Cash sales
- ☐ Refunds and claim settlements
- ☐ Sales of assets or scrap
- ☐ Interest income
- ☐ Rental income
- ☐ Customer advance payments
- ☐ New borrowings or equity contributions
- ☐ Cash received from any other source

It is crucial to include every possible type of cash receipt that could happen. The timing of each receipt is equally important.

For companies that sell on credit, collections from receivables usually represents the bulk of their cash receipts. In this case, since the cash-flow plan is done in monthly increments, estimates of monthly shipments (or sales) that increase receivables, and monthly collections that decrease receivables (and increase cash), must be made. Shipments should follow a conservative sales forecast, modified at least twice each month. Collections should be based on normal receivables turnover adjusted for any new recession-proofing techniques to be implemented.

Cash sales are self-explanatory. A retail or service company using a cash register can forecast based on recent history, adjusted for any new sales incentive programs.

Refunds include anticipated cash payments from the IRS, worker's compensation audits, state and local tax audits, downward adjustments in prepaid insurance premiums, rebates for unused airline tickets, and so on. Claim settlements usually result from winning lawsuits, insurance claims, out-of-court settlements with vendors, and recovery of previously written off receivables. If you lease out unused office, warehouse, or plant space, the cash received falls under rental income.

Of course, no plan is sacrosanct. As conditions change, new recession-proofing actions result in modified sales forecasts or other cash-generating items. The original cash-flow plan should be adjusted accordingly. Without an up-to-date picture of where cash is coming from, no amount of planning or budgeting will be effective. The dynamic nature of any business dictates continual revisions to any plan.

Cash Expenditures

The other half of the plan consists of a listing of planned cash expenditures. Obviously, the difference between cash receipts and cash expenditures in any given period shows how much cash is left over for contingencies. A cash shortfall (that is, expenditures greater than receipts), alerts you to either reduce or postpone expenditures or to get additional cash from some nonforecasted source.

The cash expenditures summary consists of five major segments.

1. Cash paid out for operating expenses—labor, materials, supplies, and overhead items

2. Cash paid for the purchase of new assets—equipment, vehicles, or space

3. Principal and interest payments on loans

4. Federal and state income taxes paid

5. Cash paid to you as salary, dividends, or other compensation plus cash paid to investors as dividends

Cash paid out for operating expenses represents the total cash to be spent each month for all costs and expenses of operating your business. Service businesses are relatively simple. Total expenditures consist of payroll and fringes, rent and other occupancy costs, selling and advertising expenses, insurance, supplies, and other miscellaneous expenses incurred every month or periodically. Many service businesses account for their transactions on the cash basis anyway, so it's not very difficult to project cash expenditures.

Purchases on credit (accounts payable) never enter the equation. Neither does inventory on hand for future production or sale. Cash expenditures for the cash-flow plan follow directly from the normal bookkeeping records or checkbook.

Manufacturing and retail businesses are a little more complicated. They must calculate cash expenditures as the amounts actually paid for purchases originally acquired on trade credit. It's the payments against accounts payable that matter, not purchases as reflected in the accounting records.

Vendor invoices are not limited to the purchase of inventory. Supplies, repairs, subcontracting, and a variety of other purchases may be made on credit. The cash payments against accounts payable are only those you expect to make each month. They may or may not have any bearing on how much was purchased.

Cash payments for the purchase of assets is self-explanatory. Again, however, if the piece of equipment or vehicle is purchased on credit extending beyond one month, a separate accounts payable schedule should be prepared in the same way as is done for purchasing inventory or supplies. Only cash payments against invoices due are included as cash expenditures.

Payments against a mortgage or a term loan is straightforward. The amount might come from an amortization table (in which case the same cash payment is made each month). Or the monthly amount may vary as the interest portion declines. In either case, projecting monthly cash payments is relatively simple.

However, planning for the payment of principal and interest on a revolving line of credit can be sticky. Assume you borrow from a bank using receivables as collateral. Further assume the bank allows a borrowing base of 85 percent of qualified receivables.

As a sale is made, the bank receives the invoice and deposits 85 percent of it in your bank account. That's a loan. As the customer pays the account, you deposit the payment in your bank account. The bank withdraws 85 percent of the deposit plus interest, leaving the balance for your discretionary use.

So far so good. You were paid for 85 percent of the sale at the time the sale was made and the other 15 percent, less interest, when the customer paid. By estimating collection time, it's fairly easy to project when the 15 percent will come in.

On the cash-flow plan, the 85 percent represents cash receipts from a bank loan, and a little later the 15 percent, less interest, is included as a cash receipt from sales. Simultaneously, the bank loan gets paid off and the interest is paid. Both of these items show up on the cash-flow plan as cash expenditures.

Complications set in, however, when you have more than one customer, shipments (sales) are made continuously throughout the month, and customer payments come in at random times. Theoretically, the bank lends against each shipment (sale). Practically, however, everything gets lumped together. Your bank balance increases or decreases by the total sales or collections each day. As long as sales continue to rise, at least 15 percent is always available for your use. But as sales decline, all of a sudden payments against the revolver loans exceed sales, and the 15 percent quickly gets wiped out.

For a company with many customers and staggered payments it is difficult to make any sense out of revolvers for cash-flow planning. About the best that can be done is to treat the multitude of loans as one, and the various paybacks as one monthly payment.

If a company is profitable, the amount paid for federal and state income taxes can frequently be higher than any other ex-

penditure. Many privately owned companies use the S corporation election to allow shareholders to pay the taxes on business
income. If you draw extra cash from the company to pay these
taxes the amounts should still be included as a business expenditure for cash-flow planning.

Taxes are the one section of the cash-flow plan that should
be prepared by an accountant. Changes in tax laws and calculations of taxable income make it virtually impossible for an
owner to calculate tax payments—unless, or course, he or she
has a strong accounting background.

Cash that you draw as salary or other compensation, or payments to outside investors as dividends should be stated
separately. In most privately held companies, the amount an
owner draws out is discretionary. Even with a formal salary or
bonus plan, you make the final decision about how much cash
to take out and when.

If one or more months show a projected cash shortfall, you
might decide to forego draws that month. In times of surplus
cash, you might decide to take extra payments. If it wasn't important to reconcile cash receipts and cash expenditures with
the balance in a bank account (covered later) the inclusion of
your compensation would be unnecessary.

Paying dividends to investors normally occurs once a year,
although they may be made more frequently. Since these expenditure have little to do with the business and since typically you
have virtually no control over whether dividends will be paid, a
one-line inclusion in the cash expenditures section should be
sufficient. If such payments are based on prior year's income
rather than fixed yields, it is probably a good idea to let your accountant calculate the amounts—at least for the current year's
plan.

Reconciliation to Bank Balance

With the cash receipts and cash expenditures sections of the
plan completed, the only remaining step is to calculate how
much extra cash will be available each month. It's a simple calculation that begins with the bank balance at the beginning of

the month, adds or subtracts the net cash during the month, and ends with the bank balance to begin the next month.

This short calculation also serves as a check on the accuracy of the cash receipts and cash expenditures projections. You will never hit it exactly, but the variance between the cash-flow plan and the actual bank balance each month should be minimal.

If it isn't, then something has gone wrong. Perhaps you missed your sales forecast or customers lagged their payments. Overtime pay might have increased or the unplanned sale of a piece of equipment occurred. Regardless of the reason for being out of balance you should probably make immediate adjustments. Allowing two months to go by with an out-of-balance cash-flow plan only leads to serious problems later on.

That finishes a very brief explanation of the cash-flow plan. As mentioned earlier, whether a business is booming or falling flat, in tough times cash must be controlled. If there isn't enough cash to meet your obligations, something must be done. A cash-flow plan is a handy tool to help anticipate when problems might hit.

As you begin to take actions to decrease costs, increase sales, sell unneeded assets, and restructure bank debt, the starting point for each of these actions is knowing how much cash you have to work with. The less excess cash generated each month, the more urgent it is to take corrective action immediately.

Most entrepreneurs who end up in bankruptcy courts do so because they do not know far enough in advance when cash shortages will occur. Although a cash-flow plan will not in itself recession-proof a business, it serves as a crucial tool for determining what actions must be taken and when they must occur.

The following chapters delve into the details of a variety of recession-proofing ideas. As programs are implemented in each area of your business, the expected cash-flow results should be summarized into the overall cash-flow plan. It is important to keep in mind that in all cases accounting niceties are just that—niceties. You need cash, not accounting entries. Ideas in succeeding chapters for generating extra cash through sales tactics, cost reductions, asset disposals, and debt restructuring exclude as much as possible confusing accounting rules and conventions.

The accent is on cash, not bookkeeping. Unfortunately, there are times when quantifying operating actions requires a modest amount of accounting terminology. Every effort has been made to keep this to a minimum and to explain terms that may be confusing.

The next chapter explores the mechanics for taking the first step toward increasing business cash—reducing costs. It presents suggestions and tips for constructing a formal cost-reduction plan. It also describes a suitable operating budget to monitor actual results against the plan. These tools provide a measure of the effectiveness of action plans and a method to monitor how much cash has been generated by them.

Chapter 2

Converting Costs to Cash

Structuring a Cost-Reduction Program

Without floor plans and the right tools a carpenter can't build a house. The same holds true for recession-proofing a business.

A cash-flow plan is similar to an architect's drawings. It establishes the ground rules for raising cash—how much is needed and when. It establishes what the end result will look like when the plan is completely implemented. It summarizes, in quantifiable terms, how each aspect of the business contributes to the finished whole.

Once the architect's drawings are approved, the next step is to develop the detailed construction plans and assemble the right tools to do the job. Similar actions hold for recession-proofing a business. Once the cash-flow plan defines how much cash is needed, what segments of the business will generate the cash, and when it must enter the company coffers, the next steps are to develop detailed plans for implementation and then to assemble the tools to monitor progress.

The primary source of new cash usually originates from reducing operating costs. A cost-reduction program represents the detailed plan to achieve this end. Operating budgets serve as the tools to monitor the progress in fulfilling these cost-reduction goals. This chapter offers ideas and recommendations for constructing this detailed plan and measuring tools.

Any company, large or small can reduce operating costs by some amount—say 10 percent to start with. During tough times luxuries and conveniences need to be abandoned. First-class airfares, second-shift janitors, redundant secretarial help, excess inventory, hour-long lunch breaks, overtime pay, routine bonuses, and noncritical travel are conveniences most companies can do without. For each dollar of cost reduced, an extra dollar gets added to the bank account.

Obviously the character of costs varies between manufacturing, distribution, service, and retail companies. The cost mix is different between each company in each industry. No universal cost reduction program can be applicable for everyone. Each must be tailored to the specific situation.

Commonalty between broad classifications does exist, however. Manufacturing companies always utilize materials and labor to produce products. Distribution companies must have space to stock products for delivery. Service companies, as a minimum, have an office and usually employ one or more technical or sales personnel. Retail operations employ sales people, and require a salesroom, store, or other facility from which to sell the wares.

It is impossible to tailor a universal cost reduction program that meets the specific needs of all companies. But a general format can be laid out. Ideas and suggestions can be proposed. Universal monitoring tools can be structured.

As we move through the preparation of cost-reduction plans, it's important to clarify that the same comments apply to cost-reduction plans as apply to cash-flow plans. No one format is better than any other. The form used must meet the requirements of the business. However, even though the format is different for each company and the details that go into a cost reduction plan vary, the methodology and approach to cost reductions remains constant.

Setting Up Controls

By their very nature, manufacturing and construction companies present opportunities for the most versatile and usually the most complex cost-reduction programs. To start with you need some type of control form, a summary sheet of paper to record current actual expenditures by type of expense and expected results from cost-reduction actions. The more you can break down and categorize each type of expenditure, the easier it is to achieve reductions.

For example, assume you have three supervisors, eighteen production employees, and an office staff of six and you have one line on the control form called *payroll*. It's impossible to measure what the effect of laying off two production workers, one clerical employee and two supervisors will be without making the detailed calculations for each class. Segregating payroll by type of employee on a control sheet makes the job much easier.

Manufacturing companies and most construction businesses incur two types of production costs.

- ☐ Material or supplies to make (or build) the product
- ☐ Payroll and employee benefits

In addition, most companies incur the following type of non-production expenses:

- ☐ Managerial and supervisory payroll
- ☐ Clerical and office payroll
- ☐ Sales payroll
- ☐ Payroll taxes and employee benefits
- ☐ Occupancy expenses—rent, property taxes, electricity, fuel
- ☐ Transportation expenses—autos, trucks, tractors, forklifts
- ☐ Maintenance and repairs expenses—supplies, contracted labor
- ☐ Protection expenses—guards, insurance, alarm systems
- ☐ Selling expenses—advertising, public relations, printing, travel, entertainment

☐ Administrative expenses—data processing, office supplies, professional fees

Although the proportionate importance of each expense classification varies with the type of business, they all play a role in keeping companies functioning. Quite naturally, nearly all expenses appear absolutely essential to the conduct of a business. No one intentionally spends more than necessary to get the job done. Reducing essential purchases and payroll hurts as much as pulling teeth.

Unfortunately, to translate tough times into opportunities for future growth, some hurt must be inflicted. There is no easy way out. Costs must be reduced.

Production Costs
Since production costs usually represent the largest cost category and the most difficult to trim back, this is a good place to start. Begin by listing the production costs applicable to your business. Perhaps the following groupings might fit your operation. If not, design your own categories.

1. Production materials

   a. Raw materials

   b. Product supplies—shipping containers

   c. Process/equipment supplies

   d. Finished product

2. Production payroll

   a. Direct workers

   b. Support/assistance workers

   c. Nondirect activities

   d. Supervision

3. Employee benefits

   a. Payroll taxes/worker's compensation

   b. Group insurance and pension

   c. Tools, meals, day care, other miscellaneous benefits

   d. Bonuses/incentive payments

Next, insert the amount of cash that was paid out for each of these categories last month and estimate the amounts for next month. The same rule about using cash payments against supplier invoices as discussed in chapter 1 applies here. On the *finished product* line, only cash expenditures for products to be resold (as a retailer) should be included. The cost of producing finished product is reflected in purchased material and payroll categories.

Production payroll includes all employees directly associated with manufacturing the product. Only the total payroll for each category of employee should be inserted; not the amounts paid to individual employees. Be sure to include monthly amounts for those paid weekly, biweekly, or semimonthly.

Payroll taxes, worker's compensation premiums, and group insurance payments should be the same as last month. Payments might be made semi-annually or annually to a pension fund or retirement plan. In that case, note the time frame on the pension line.

Nonproduction Expenses
Payroll for nonproduction personnel should be grouped by major classification—supervisory, clerical, sales, and so on. It also helps to include payroll taxes and employee benefits under each caption. This makes it easier to judge the impact of cost reduction actions. Your own salary and other compensation should obviously be excluded.

Cash payments for such nonproduction expenses as telephone, advertising, maintenance supplies, and legal fees will probably vary erratically month to month. If expenditures from last month do not reflect normal monthly payments, either an average or a reasonable estimate should be used as the starting point.

Clearly, if the complexities in your business are minimal, you don't need to worry about a complicated control sheet to know what is going on. Just record expected cost reductions on a piece of paper and be done with it. But do record them. This discipline makes the effort more formal, and formal plans are always easier to implement than mental pictures of what you want.

Cost-Reduction Objectives

Once you have a handle on actual expenditures, it's time to move on to structuring the cost-reduction program. Once again, every company is different and no single plan works for everyone. The suggestions that follow are just that—suggestions. Obviously, you have to come up with those reductions that fit your business.

Certain rules should be followed, however, to ensure the effectiveness of a cost-reduction program.

Rules For An Effective Cost-Reduction Program

1. Cost-reduction actions must be quantifiable. That is, the result of the action must be translatable into dollar reductions in one or more expense categories.

2. The cash savings from cost-reduction actions should be in reverse proportion to time. That is, the greatest savings should be shortly after the action is implemented. As time progresses, cash savings either disappear or continue at a decreasing pace.

3. Actions that will have a major effect on cash within six months should be given priority.

4. Projected savings from cost-reductions should be formally recorded in a format appropriate for your business.

5   The cash savings resulting from cost reduction actions must be measurable. That is, once a cost reduction is quantified, as in rule 1, a method must be implemented to measure whether or not the action resulted in the expected savings.

6. If cash savings are expected to be realized in increments over time or if the cost-reduction action itself will be implemented over time, milestones should be established against which to measure incremental savings.

7. One individual must have responsibility for seeing that the action is implemented. In a one-person business, obviously this must be the owner. If you have several employees, then someone other than yourself should be assigned the responsibility even though you manage the project.

8. Cost-reduction steps should be carefully chosen to inflict the least amount of long-term harm on the business and to hurt the fewest people.

Several clients have tried to implement cost-reduction programs without following these simple rules. None resulted in the amount of cash savings expected. Most programs were abandoned before they were completed.

One reason they didn't work was that the planned cost reductions were so general that they could not be quantified and measured. Milestones could not be set and personnel responsible for implementing action steps became discouraged by the apparent lack of progress. Clients cited a more important reason, however: that the selected cost reductions caused more harm than good to the business. A perfect example occurred with a client in Iowa.

Jim owned a farm implement dealership close to Waterloo, Iowa. For eight years sales climbed and Jim added several capable sales people, field service personnel, a purchasing manager, and a bookkeeping department—twelve people in total. When the bottom fell out of the agricultural equipment market, Jim decided a stringent cost-reduction program was the only solution for saving the business. He retained me to help structure the program.

We diligently set up the appropriate format to record existing expenditures. Jim, his sales manager, purchasing manager, and bookkeeper came up with eighteen areas of costs that could be reduced. I cautioned that this seemed like a lot for such a small business but Jim was adamant. I also cautioned that he should set up a measuring system, such as operating budgets, to track each action as savings were realized. He didn't have time for such a mundane administrative task.

Jim assigned each of his three managers six action steps and instructed them to go to it. In four months a total of three cost reductions were implemented: a shelving of the company's effective advertising program, a cutback in sales personnel from four to three, and restrictions on long-distance phone calls. Within six months the sales manager quit, citing the disintegration of his customer base. He blamed the cost-reduction moves.

Typical Production Cost Reductions

When I propose to clients that a cost-reduction program should be implemented as one means of increasing cash-flow, they invariably ask the same question: "What costs can I cut that will make any significant difference without damaging the business over the long haul?"

Unfortunately no simple answer exists. What works in one company almost certainly will not work in another. Your personal objectives, qualifications of personnel, type and size of business, market conditions, and many other factors are all unique to your company. However, the same approach can be applied in most businesses, even though the details vary.

Aside from reducing the cost of borrowed money, which is dealt with in chapter 9, nearly every business has one or more of the following categories of expenditures against which a cost reduction program can be implemented:

1. Expenditures for the purchase of material, products, or supplies that will either be resold, converted to other products that are sold, or used in performing a service that is sold.

2. Expenditures for materials, supplies, and outside services that are not converted into sales but required to support other activities of the business.

3. Expenditures for people.

4. Expenditures to maintain a facility from which business can be conducted.

5. Expenditures to comply with government requirements.

Let's look at a few ideas that might apply in each of these categories.

Materials and Supplies
Production supervisors always want to have plenty of material on hand so they won't run short during the production cycle. The same can be said for store managers. They know that if the goods aren't in stock when a customer wants to buy, the sale falls through.

When business is booming the tendency is always to stock more than enough inventory. As everyone knows, you can't sell from an empty basket. But having enough material on hand to meet customer demand compared to having an excess in stock so you'll never run out are two quite different conditions.

In addition to the glowing reports we have all heard about the superior productivity of Japanese workers and their strong work ethic, one of the real contributions Japanese manufacturers have made to the producers and sellers of the world is a purchasing concept called "just in time" deliveries, commonly referred to as JIT.

This doctrine stipulates that a manufacturer, distributor, or retailer will not take delivery of materials until they are actually needed. Storerooms are stocked "just in time" to meet production schedules or to make the sale.

JIT purchasing has grown in popularity over the past decade. Most giant corporations, including some of the largest—GE, the automobile manufacturers, the aerospace companies, AT & T, and Sears—now mandate the policy throughout their divisions and branches.

Shifting to JIT purchasing is an effective cost-reduction action. A one-time cash saving has amounted to as much as 25 percent of purchased inventory for many companies. And any company can use JIT. The only requirements are to (1) understand exactly what inventory you must have to maintain customer demand levels and (2) assign someone the responsibility of making sure orders are placed and deliveries received to match this level.

Another potential cost-reduction step could be to reduce the amount of wasted supplies and materials. Even with the best inventory control system, employees tend to be careless about supplies. How often do we fill wastebaskets with computer paper, letterhead, and drafting paper to be carted off to the dump? Why not use the back sides for scratch paper and internal memos instead of buying more letterhead and paper tablets?

Machine oil, janitorial supplies, computer printer ribbons, out-of-date catalogs and price sheets are other supplies that tend to be wasted. A conscientious effort to eliminate waste can result in substantial cost reductions.

And what about manufacturing scrap? Many companies pay to have scrap removed from the premises to a local dump without realizing that everything has some value for someone. A cost-reduction effort to search out legitimate buyers for scrap could yield cash savings in two ways: by eliminating the cost of hauling it away and by selling it.

Expenditures for outside services should also be examined closely. Do you really need equipment maintenance contracts or is it cheaper to pay as you go for repairs? Relatively new equipment shouldn't break down. Why pay for expensive maintenance contracts with little likelihood of major repairs?

Legal fees are another cost companies can usually reduce. Corporate lawyers love to have monthly retainer contracts to cover calls and advice on inconsequential matters, and then charge extra for preparing lawsuits or for court appearances. Do you really need to have a lawyer on standby? Try solving routine problems yourself and use lawyers only for major legal actions.

Accounting and audit fees fall into the same category. If a bank or other outside party doesn't require quarterly or annual audits, why go to the expense of certification when accounting reviews would suffice? If you have accounting personnel on staff and they are not included in cost-reduction layoffs, why not prepare payroll, sales, use, property, and other tax returns within the company rather than paying extra for a CPA firm to do the job?

Many other possibilities exist for reducing expenditures for operating expenses, purchased materials, and supplies. Putting a little effort into examining the internal policies for buying, storing, and using materials and outside services generally results in cost reductions not recognized when business was booming. The president of J & R Locknut Company was thoroughly surprised with his results.

Bob Shimmelt, owner and president of J & R Locknut Company realized that with business turning down he had to do something to keep costs in line. Bob was a terrific salesman but always had difficulty working with numbers. With only four people on the payroll he was at a loss about how to cut costs. Five years earlier a consultant had set up a computerized inventory stocking system for the J & R primary warehouse. As the reserve stock of any part dropped below a predetermined level, automatic purchase orders were triggered.

Bob's accountant felt this system resulted in excess inventory but kept her mouth shut knowing that Bob had paid a sizable amount for the system. When I was called in to take a look at potential cost reductions, I agreed with her. We suggested that Bob throw out the computer system and return to 3 x 5 cards as inventory records. I further recommended bringing the stock levels down another 20 percent. A new supplier ten blocks away could supply emergency parts within four hours. This reduction in inventory resulted in a one-time cash generation of nearly $20,000.

Personnel

A company employing more than ten people can generally find a way to get by with at least one or two fewer. The 10 percent reduction rule of thumb is a good place to begin. Although during tough times the tendency is to layoff people not directly associated with either producing or selling products or services, this often damages a company over the long haul. Personnel responsible for purchasing, accounting, quality assurance, advertising, data processing, engineering, and human relations activities perform functions crucial to the long-term health of a company.

Another mistake commonly made when there are only a few employees is to assume that a manager or the owner can adequately perform additional activities. Therefore laying off a bookkeeper, a sales person, or clerical help will save money. Certainly one person can perform several different jobs. Owners of companies with no employees prove it every day. At the same time, by diverting your attention from selling or production to less critical activities, you inevitably hurt the business in the long run.

Exactly the opposite also happens: making the assumption that all employees perform critical jobs and therefore that no one can be laid off. During tough times this can be a fatal error, as a client in the auto repair business learned the hard way.

> Jake owned a string of three auto repair garages in a suburb of Philadelphia. Expanding the business from his original one bay shop with no employees, Jake now employed twelve full-time mechanics and two administrative clerks. Normally when a recession hit, people kept repairing the old jalopy one more time rather than buying new cars. But this time around business fell off. Several mechanics spent two or three hours each day cleaning the shops rather than working on cars. I advised Jake that if he kept spending more money than he took in, his cash reserves would soon dry up.
>
> Jake was obstinate. He insisted that good mechanics were hard to find and he would rather waste some money now on nonproductive time than let mechanics go and then have to re-hire them when business turned up. If Jake's cash wasn't disappearing so fast, this would have been a hard argument to dispel. But it was.

Within four months Jake couldn't pay his withholding taxes. In another two months the landlord threatened foreclosure. Within a year, Jake sold his rapidly declining business for substantially less than a profitable operation would have brought. A well-conceived cost-reduction program beginning with a reduction in employees might have saved the business; but Jake will never know for sure.

A good way to determine the right number of employees for a business is to relate it to sales. Many trade associations maintain statistics compiled over the years from member companies. Most include ratios of the number of people to sales, or payroll cost to sales. These statistics are averages and are probably not specifically applicable to your company. But they serve as a good starting point to judge if employee cost reductions should be seriously considered.

Possibilities for employee cost reductions other than direct layoffs might include the following actions:

1. Not replacing an employee when he or she quits. Assign these responsibilities to existing employees.

2. Encouraging early retirement for older employees and not replacing them.

3. Extending health-care coverage or other benefits in exchange for an across-the-board reduction in wages.

4. Implementing an employee cost-reduction suggestion system with noncash rewards.

Chapter 3 examines a variety of approaches to increasing cash-flow through employee cost reductions in addition to these four.

Occupancy Cost Reductions

Every company occupies some type of plant, warehouse, or office space from which to conduct the business. The space itself is either leased or owned by the company or the owner. In addition to rent payments or mortgage payments, property taxes may be paid separately.

Every business pays for some type of utility service: electricity, water, and fuel. In addition to utilities, most businesses carry property and casualty insurance to protect against fire, wind, rain, vandalism, and theft.

At first glance it might appear that little can be done to reduce the cash expenditures for these costs. By applying creative ingenuity, however, you should be able to find cost reductions in occupancy expenses as well as purchases and payroll.

Electricity, water, and fuel costs can usually be reduced just by being more careful. Turn out the lights when a room isn't in use. Make sure water taps and toilets don't leak. Maintain thermostat settings within a wider band. Restrict air conditioning and heat to those areas occupied by people (as opposed to storage areas).

In a manufacturing operation, avoid repeated equipment start-ups and shut-downs that require excess electric current. Shut down the company swimming pool (if you are fortunate enough to have one). Charge employees a nominal fee for using company exercise facilities, vehicles, and other convenience benefits requiring electricity, water, or fuel.

Many companies seldom review their property and casualty coverage. They let the insurance salesman or broker determine changes in coverage. But insurance companies are notorious for increasing coverage, and hence premiums, periodically without first informing the policyholder. They justify this by claiming that inflation drives up the cost of replacing property and therefore increased coverage is in your best interest.

Fine. Except that in tough times perhaps you are willing to assume this risk yourself. Maybe even set up a self-insurance reserve. In most cases, a company should be able to reduce insurance premiums either by cutting the coverage recommended by the insurance carrier or by going the self-insurance route.

Reducing building rental payments may be impossible. However, in tough times, many buildings go unoccupied and this drives the rental market down. It's certainly possible that a landlord might be amenable to renegotiating lease terms in a depressed market, especially for an office or warehouse.

Regardless of how inflexible occupancy costs seem to be, an active cost-reduction program almost always nets cash savings. Once achieved, these cost savings frequently become permanent changes. As business conditions improve, owners seem reticent to go back to previous, inefficient habits. They prove to themselves that they can survive and prosper without the fat.

Clients have told me over and over again that they never realized how extravagant they had become until a stringent cost-reduction program was implemented. When they see how much extra cash can be generated, few return to their old ways.

Chapter 4 highlights additional ways to cut occupancy costs as well as other "fixed" costs.

Compliance Payments

Payments to comply with government, bank, and other outside regulators remain more or less immune to cost reductions. Taxes of all varieties must be paid on time to escape penalties. Expenditures to meet safety or environmental requirements are difficult to avoid. Licenses, permits, and worker's compensation insurance must be retained to stay in business. It is difficult to dodge payments for imprinted bank checks, deposit lockboxes, and other charges mandated by banks.

On the other hand, an effort can be made to keep these costs at a minimum. Challenging unemployment and worker's compensation claims can keep these premiums as low as possible. Negotiating with OSHA and EPA auditors to delay implementation of compliance programs might save cash in the short run. Changing banks, or threatening to change, could result in significantly reduced charges for bank services.

As with other operating costs, a cost-reduction program for compliance payments can effect real savings. They might not be as great as those realized with other expenses, but every dollar saved ends up as extra cash to work with.

Once a list of cost-reduction possibilities has been completed, the expected savings should be recorded on the cost-reduction control sheet. A full description of what actions will be taken by whom to achieve the reduction should be included.

The time frame within which the savings will be realized should also be established. If it's a one-shot cash savings, record the month in which it will occur. If it's a continuing savings, indicate over what period of time it will occur and in what monthly increments.

It's critical to formalize a cost-reduction program by quantifying expected results. Totals from this time-sequenced program become integral parts of the overall cash-flow plan established in chapter 1. Without a well-conceived, documented, and quantified cost-reduction program a cash-flow plan is incomplete.

All assumptions supporting how, when, and why each cost-reduction effort will be implemented should be documented. A loose-leaf notebook serves this purpose well. Sheets can be added or deleted as the program progresses and assumptions change.

As mentioned earlier, recession-proofing is dynamic. Strategies, tactics, plans, and programs keep changing over time as new information emerges and market conditions vary. Both the cash-flow plan and its supporting cost-reduction program serve as the starting point. To become working tools, they must be adjusted as changing conditions become known.

Measuring Progress

For more than fifty years people have praised and criticized the effectiveness of budgets. The debate has no end. Budgets work great for those who like to live their lives or operate their business according to a plan. Budgets don't work for those who prefer extemporaneous actions.

The fundamental principle underlying all the ideas and recommendations in this book is that recession-proofing a company requires following a plan. In the sense that budgets are plans, one could surmise that these recession-proofing methods require implementing a complex—and perhaps meaningless—budget system. Nothing could be further from the truth.

Operating budgets are introduced at this point in the recession-proofing process merely to define one tool for measuring progress against the cost-reduction program. For this purpose, a brief explanation of the construction and use of operating budgets will suffice.

Business budgets come in a variety of forms. Many very complex. For purposes of measuring cash savings, a very simple set of operating budgets does the trick. A separate budget should be prepared for each person in the organization assigned the responsibility of implementing a cost reduction.

A larger organization might have one budget for each department manager and perhaps a sub-budget for each supervisor reporting to managers—although this tends to be overkill. In smaller organizations with fewer people and less formal lines of authority three budgets should suffice: one for the production activity (if any); one for sales and marketing expenses; and one for administrative, occupancy, and other supporting expenses.

Figure 2-1 illustrates how an operating budget for the latter category might look.

<u>Figure 2-1</u>

OPERATING BUDGET
Administrative and Occupancy Expenses

For the month of January, 19xx, and year to date

Year to Date				January		
Over (Under)	Budget	Actual	Expense	Actual	Budget	Over (Under)
			PAYROLL			
_____			Salaries/wages	_____		
_____			Payroll taxes	_____		
_____			Employee benefits	_____		
_____			Other	_____		
_____			Total payroll	_____		
			EXPENSES			
_____			Supplies	_____		
_____			Telephone	_____		
_____			Travel	_____		
_____			Entertainment	_____		
_____			Professional fees	_____		
_____			Other taxes	_____		
_____			Other expenses	_____		
_____			Total expenses	_____		

OCCUPANCY

_____	Rent (building)	_____
_____	Rent (equipment)	_____
_____	Property taxes	_____
_____	Insurance	_____
_____	Electricity	_____
_____	Water	_____
_____	Fuel (oil, gas, coal)	_____
_____	Other expenses	_____
_____	Total occupancy	_____

TOTAL EXPENSES

When inserting expenditures in the actual columns, disregard everything you may have learned about bookkeeping. Only cash payments should be used. If invoices have been received but not yet paid, the amount doesn't get inserted until payment. Every month the actual expenditures are inserted in the month column and added to the previous month's year-to-date balance.

The month and year-to-date budget amounts should be taken from the cost-reduction control sheet. If a specific line item has no planned reduction scheduled for a given month, it should be left blank.

As you begin working with these operating budgets, it won't take long to see clearly whether the cost-reduction program is working. If year-to-date actual amounts continue to run in excess of expected results, obviously the cost reductions—and hence the excess cash—you planned for are not happening. Something is wrong: corrective action must be taken.

Without your close and immediate attention to the progress of planned cost reductions, the program won't work. Recession-proofing is a continuous management task. Not a one-shot exercise. Measuring actual progress against expected results must be your responsibility. Time and again attempts have been made to delegate this responsibility and it never works. For example:

> Before he left for a six-week vacation in Europe, Jack Plagett, owner of Acelet Heating and Plumbing Distributors, told his office manager to be sure everyone put through the action plans agreed upon. When Jack returned, expenditures were higher than when he had left. No cost reductions had been implemented, and in fact, cash-flow had deteriorated.

Or in another case:

> Alice Johnson ran a flower and plant boutique. She developed a cost-reduction program to yield an additional $15,000 cash for the third quarter. When Alice took her annual buying trip to Mexico and the Caribbean she put her bookkeeper in charge of implementing the plan. When she returned, the bookkeeper quickly informed Alice that although she had tried hard to follow directions, she couldn't figure out how to buy fewer cut flowers and still have enough on hand to sell.

Abdicating responsibility for the implementation of any part of the recession-proofing process just won't work—especially a cost-reduction segment. If you're not serious about doing it now, then postpone the actions until you have time to manage the program. Otherwise it's a waste of time and effort.

Managing Cost Reductions in Family Businesses

Managing the program in a company with one or two employees is much easier than in larger companies—unless these employees happen to be family members. Then it can become a nightmare! Instructing your spouse or children to stop spending money or to change the way they are doing something can be a frustrating experience.

Your husband or wife always seems to have their own way of doing a task that they believe is clearly superior to yours and will always bring better results. Children may follow directions while you are around, but they also tend to think and act on their own. And of course, you have little recourse if they do disobey. Have you ever tried firing a spouse or one of your children?

Several years ago I owned a small tax service. I personally interviewed every client, mostly in their offices, and then turned half of the material over to my wife. We both prepared the returns and checked each other's work. During a particularly severe recession in the area, I decided to cut automobile expenses by asking clients to come to my office for interviews. No one objected and the tax season was progressing smoothly.

Then I became ill and was hospitalized. My wife took over the interviewing process. When I paid bills at the end of the month, the gasoline credit card charges shocked me. When querying my wife, her response was, "Well, it was hard for those people to come to the office, so I decided to go to theirs." So much for cost reductions!

One way to get younger family members to do what you want in the business is to let it be known that the action is required for "tax purposes." Everyone finds it difficult to argue with the IRS.

This chapter has reviewed the basics of setting up and managing the cost-reduction section of the cash-flow puzzle. After laying out the total program, the differences between the current and projected monthly cash savings becomes the new planned cash expenditures. These monthly totals are then transferred, by expense category, to the cash-flow plan in chapter 1.

Before leaving the subject of reducing operating costs, it might be helpful to review some of the additional cost savings that could be implemented. The following two chapters examine possibilities in the personnel and administration areas.

Chapter 3

Headcount Headaches
Reducing Personnel Costs

Tough times hurt. As tactics for improving cash-flow, tough actions to reduce costs and to improve sales go hand in hand. The highest operating costs are the ones to tackle first; and in many companies, the highest costs relate to personnel. Cash paid for wages and for employee benefits frequently exceed any other operating cost with the exception of income taxes.

We all know that capable people are hard to find. When we do assemble a contingent of technically qualified, honest, intelligent personnel we want to keep them. We also want to keep them reasonably content in their jobs. The thought of losing key employees and having to recruit all over again can be shattering. Furthermore, personnel layoffs hurt. Employees get hurt and a caring owner gets hurt. Still, to survive in tough times it's usually necessary to look hard at reducing personnel costs.

Many owners find personnel costs not only the biggest operating expense but also the quickest to reduce. Countless small businesses find it more practical, albeit painful, to reduce personnel costs than to slice advertising programs, selling expenses, maintenance costs, and other expenses essential to keep the business alive.

Personnel cost reductions result from four types of action. You can:

1. Layoff employees and shift work loads to those remaining

2. Substitute lesser-cost employees for those currently employed

3. Reduce cash payments for employee benefits

4. Replace a portion of cash wages with noncash incentives

The choice of one or a combination of these options is controlled to a large extent by the type of business and by how many people are on the payroll. A consulting business that sells employee hours can't reduce the number of personnel without reducing sales. A public relations business consisting of the owner and no employees obviously must look elsewhere for cost reductions. Conversely, a machine shop employing five direct labor people, two salesmen, and three office personnel can implement any one or all of these actions.

Chapter 2 suggested several possibilities for payroll cost reductions. This chapter looks at additional options. The same principle of quantifying cash savings and utilizing the cost reduction plan described in chapter 2 applies to all cost-reduction actions regardless of the specific expense category.

Reducing the Number of Employees

Several possibilities exist for achieving cash savings by reducing the number of people on the payroll. Three cost elements are involved: wages paid, payroll taxes, and employee benefits. For every wage dollar cut, payroll taxes and employee benefits are reduced proportionately.

Payroll taxes consist of an employer's share of social security (FICA) taxes, state and federal taxes for unemployment compensation, and special earnings taxes imposed by city, township, county, state, or other governmental unit. The FICA tax rate is 7.65 percent in 1991, of which a portion is used to fund medicare insurance. The tax is payable on all individuals' wages up to a total of $53,400.

The total tax rate for federal unemployment compensation (FUTA) is 6.2 percent on wages up to a maximum of $7,000. Because most employers are allowed credits against this rate from state unemployment programs, the net FUTA rate is .8 percent, except when a state uses credit reductions.

Tax rates under state unemployment laws vary all over the lot. (Many states call this "insurance" rather than a tax, but a rose is still a rose.) The more claims against the fund, the higher an employer's rate. The total unemployment rate—federal and state combined—often exceeds 6.2 percent. In some states it ranges as high as 10 percent when disability insurance and other obscure add-ons are included.

As a minimum, payroll taxes alone add another 13.85 percent to wage payments up to $7,000 and 7.65 percent on those up to $53,400. Extraneous local taxes make it much more in some locales.

Premium payments for worker's compensation insurance also vary by state. Occupation designation and claims against an employer's fund determine the amount paid in. Payments for employees in dangerous occupations can hit $10,000 or more per year. Payments for office workers can be less than $1,000 per year.

Group medical and life insurance premiums, pension and profit-sharing payments, education assistance, day-care expenses, physical fitness facilities, medical examinations, and many other benefits add significantly to personnel costs. Payments for holidays, vacations, sick leave, jury duty, armed forces leave, and other nonproductive time adds another big slice.

As a general rule, it is not uncommon in companies with twenty-five or more employees and union representation to add 50 to 70 percent to actual wages paid to arrive at the actual out-of-pocket payments for employees. Even businesses employing two or three office personnel can easily estimate a 25 to 30 percent add-on.

It's easy to see why employee layoffs have become a popular cost reduction action, in spite of the hurt inflicted. Few other actions save as much immediate cash as layoffs. Of course, severance pay must be subtracted in arriving at the net savings.

Employee layoffs inevitably cause confusion in a company. Assuming the tasks performed by the ex-employee continue, the big question is, "Who will do the work now?" Some of the work goes away as business drops. Other tasks are probably not essential and can be stopped without any impact.

It's human nature for most people to feel that they are fully occupied and cannot take on any additional assignments. We tend to use this ploy to justify our jobs. Whether or not we really work eight hours a day remains in question!

With the exception of highly technical activities most people have the time and the ability to pick up an ex-employee's critical work, whether they admit it or not. The luxury of employee "prima donnas" can't be tolerated during tough times.

Another option, at least for certain types of work, is to farm it out to an independent contractor. Several bookkeeping tasks, janitorial and security jobs, compliance reporting, data processing, and a host of other activities can frequently be performed at lower cost and even more efficiently by an independent contractor.

I owned a small machine shop that went into a tailspin after losing a major contract. Costs had to be cut and cut fast. In the accounting department we employed a bookkeeper and two payroll clerks; one to calculate and write payroll and the other to record labor hours by job. When we lost the contract, I immediately gave notice to the two payroll clerks, much to the chagrin of the bookkeeper. After all, it was her empire I was decimating.

I hired the bank next door to calculate and write the weekly payroll for a monthly fee approximating one-fourth of the salaries and benefits paid to the two payroll clerks. As a by-product, I worked out a system with the bank's data processing department to provide weekly summaries of labor hours by job—at a token charge. By using this outside service bureau in place of two employees I saved nearly $3,000 per month, or $36,000 per year! That, plus other cost reductions and marketing actions saved the company.

By the next time I had to look at severe personnel reductions (this time in a small retail establishment) I had developed the short evaluation worksheet in figure 3-1 to help decide what employee-independent contractor tradeoffs made sense.

<u>Figure 3-1</u>

Evaluation of Employee/Independent Contractor Tradeoffs

Potential Employee to Be Laid Of	Wages and Benefits	Monthly Major Duties

Independent Contractors
Capable of Performing These Duties

Name	Address	Phone Number

Bids received

Monthly cost _____

Pickup and delivery (yes or no) _____

Duration of contract _____

References (at least three)

Name/Address

_____

_____

_____

Most of my small business clients have been reticent to consider personnel layoffs except in very severe emergencies. Whereas larger corporations tend to look at layoffs as a first step in reducing operating costs, entrepreneurs seem to feel differently about their employees. Most have a genuine concern about their employees' welfare. Why more owners don't tell this to their employees remains a mystery. When consulting with smaller clients about cost reduction programs I have used the questionnaire in figure 3-2 to assess the advisability of specific layoffs.

Figure 3-2

Employee Evaluation Questionnaire

Name of Employee   Position

_____   _____

Length of time with company   _____

Monthly wage   _____

Benefit percentage   _____

    Total monthly expense   _____

In a special interest group?		Attitude toward company?	
Race	_____	Outstanding	_____
Sex	_____	Adequate	_____
Age	_____	Poor	_____
Welfare	_____		
Gov't. subsidy	_____	Good work habits?	
Union	_____	Always	_____
Other	_____	Usually	_____
		Seldom	_____

Does he/she have good rapport with other employees? _____

What are the most crucial jobs he/she performs? List.

_____

_____

_____

Who else in the company can get these jobs done?

_____

_____

_____

What does the company lose by moving the task to someone else?

_____

_____

_____

Are there independent contractors available to do the task? _____

Who?

_____

_____

_____

At what cost?

_____

Will you offer this employee severance pay? How much? _____

How much vacation/holiday pay does he/she have accumulated? _____

How readily can this employee get another job?

Easily	_____
With some effort	_____
Unlikely in a short time	_____

Decision Weighting Summary

Net cash savings	_____
Effect on employee	_____
Effect on other employees	_____
Yes or no	
If yes, when	_____

Substitute Lower-Cost Employees

Another form of personnel cost reduction that works for some companies is to substitute lower-paid employees for higher-paid ones. This still involves layoffs of those with higher salaries although some employees might take early retirement if asked. Of course all the hurt and disruption accompanying layoffs will still be felt. However, by substituting one employee for another, technical or other tasks not susceptible to outside contracting can still be performed without damage to the company.

One example of substituting lower- for higher-paid employees worked at the New Jersey sales and distribution center of a valve manufacturing client. This client had been in business for over forty years. The New Jersey center was staffed with eighteen people: seven in sales and warehouse management, a controller and four clerks, two truck drivers, and four field service mechanics.

The seven managers had been with the company for years. The lowest annual salary was $50,000. Four were near retirement age. All four field service mechanics were in their twenties and thirties earning $30,000 on average.

As part of a cost-reduction program, I suggested asking two sales managers and one warehouse manager to take early retirement and then to promote three field service people to the open slots. The company hired new field service replacements fairly easily. This maneuver added nearly $75,000 to the company's cash-flow during the first year.

This example might appear to be unusual, but it really isn't. If some employees are approaching retirement age, and a pension plan is in place, the risk of promoting someone to fill the shoes of another taking early retirement can have a mushrooming effect. It saves cash. It reinforces employee morale by promoting from within. It encourages older employees to enjoy retirement years when they might otherwise feel an obligation to the company to remain working.

Substitution works almost as well when no one else in the organization has the ability to immediately fill the shoes of the retiring employee. A temporary, part-time independent contractor can fill the gap (most likely at a lesser cost) until a permanent replacement can either be trained within the company or recruited.

There are literally thousands of highly qualified managers, either out of work or retired, who are available to fill management slots temporarily. And it's easy to hire them as independent contractors, not employees, and save the payroll taxes and benefit costs. The best results from this action are usually realized when the employee leaving the company holds a management position (e.g., such as chief engineer, sales manager, controller, or contracts administrator). Recruiting part-time help for jobs further down the organization is more difficult, but certainly not impossible.

Management consultants practicing on their own can also fill positions on a temporary basis. I have taken several extended-term management engagements when my other business has been slow and they have all worked well for both parties. Several other consultants in my consortium also do this work occasionally.

Since the work is temporary and usually requires a limited number of days each week, the cost is nearly always less than for a full-time employee. Most consultants willing to do this work will negotiate a fixed price per month for a set number of days of work. Few are willing to commit to more than one or two months however. If you still need him or her after that, you can always renegotiate.

The following guidelines can be helpful in structuring the right contract for part-time management help.

Contract Guidelines For Part-time Management

1. Time: not less than one month and not more than six months

2. Cancellation clause: cancellation by either party with thirty days written notice

3. Responsibilities of part-time manager:

   a. Supervise department employees

   b. Make recommendations for improving operations

   c. Submit timely reports as required

   d. Follow all company policies

   e. Perform all work in a professional manner

4. Authority of part-time manager:

   a. Included in written instructions, job parameters, and consent by business owner at beginning of engagement

5. Responsibilities of company:

   a. Abide by the authority granted the manager at the beginning of engagement

   b. Support decisions by manager as long as they do not conflict with mutually accepted responsibilities and company policy

   c. Make payment for services in a timely fashion

   d. Provide adequate working conditions for the manager

   e. Inform all personnel of the authority and responsibility of temporary manager and explain why he/she is there

   f. Provide a tax Form 1099 to temporary manager within two months of completion of engagement or calendar year end, whichever is earlier

6. Fees: Manager submits invoice for negotiated fee within three days of the end of each month. Payment by company within ten days of receipt of invoice

7. Hold harmless: Company will hold temporary manager harmless from any liability or damages resulting from the performance of the aforementioned duties, providing manager follows all written company policies

Local Chamber of Commerce or Small Business Administration offices can often be helpful in suggesting qualified retirees or individual consultants for this type of part-time work. As can banks and larger law firms.

The best reference usually comes from other companies in your area. Circulate what you need and chances are good someone will point you to a person qualified to do the job.

Cut Cash Payments for Employee Benefits

Worker's compensation and payroll taxes cannot be touched because of prevailing state and federal laws but other benefits can be changed as conditions warrant. Although reducing employee benefits such as group insurance, pension plan contributions, educational assistance, and day care usually meets with as much resistance as wage reductions, companies find ways around the objections. It is not uncommon when times get tough to ask employees to share the cash crunch burden. However, employee acquiescence is crucial to making these reductions work.

One approach might be to increase employee contributions toward group insurance premiums. If the company pays the entire bill now, ask the employees to pay part. If they already pay part of the premium, ask for a greater contribution. When it comes to saving jobs, and insurance coverage along with the jobs, employees usually agree to help.

Payments to employee pension plans can also be trimmed back. If your company uses Simplified Employee Plans (SEP) or 401(K) plans, either reduce the current year's contributions or eliminate them entirely for a period of time.

Other employee benefits can also be temporarily abated or reduced. Try to get employees to forego educational assistance, day-care reimbursements, and annual physical examinations for a temporary period. Assess fees or donations for the use of company facilities for physical fitness activities, charitable group events, or employee social gatherings.

Holidays and vacations normally amount to the biggest piece of the benefit pie and are more difficult to cut. On the other hand, if it comes to saving jobs, employees are often willing to delay vacation plans for a year or two. Of course, if you take this tact be prepared to offer compensatory time or pay at a later date. This approach worked for Mary Sue when she needed to reduce costs in her architectural drafting firm.

> As business dropped off, Mary Sue knew she either had to trim costs or lay off three draftsmen. She approached the eight drafting engineers on her payroll and asked for help. After explaining that it looked like the drop in business would probably continue for at least two years but that over the long haul

work should pick up again, all eight employees agreed to forego their three-week vacations for two years and reduce their holidays from twelve to nine. In exchange, Mary Sue promised a 10 percent increase at the end of the two-year period. Although the cash savings only lasted two years, it was enough to get Mary Sue over a rough period.

Replace Cash Wages with Noncash Incentives
In some circumstances it is possible to reduce personnel cash expenditures by substituting noncash benefits for part of the wage base. Structured properly, such incentives might be taxfree to the employee, tax deductible by the company, and save cash—all at the same time. This arrangement is the reverse of cutting employee benefits. In this case, increase benefits in exchange for reduced wages or in lieu of annual wage increases.

Noncash incentives work especially well in companies with very few employees—say up to five. The scheme also seems appropriate for companies employing professionals—engineers, health-care workers, architects, and so on. Some noncash incentives involve actual cash expenditures by the company but in most cases the cash expended is much less than the wage (plus benefits) tradeoff.

The following are ten examples of noncash benefits that companies have used in lieu of cash wages.

Noncash Employee Benefits

1. Free use of company-owned vacation facilities (e.g., cabin, lodge, villa, yacht)

2. Take spouse along on business trips

3. Donations of company property to employee's favorite charity

4. Free use of company exercise facility

5. Supplemental health insurance through a self-insured plan

6. Free use of company property/facility (for businesses that sell services or products usable by the employee, such as hotels, restaurants, bars, tax services, health care, transportation, and so on)

7. Options to purchase company stock

8. Shares in limited partnerships for development projects

9. Free training in new, nonjob related skills such as tax return preparation, printing, foreign language, personal computer applications, and so on

10. Free use of company tickets for sporting events

Offering employees a share of the company in exchange for reduced wages (or in lieu of increases) can be one of the best, readily acceptable noncash incentives. Psychologically, most people want to be entrepreneurs. Owning part of the boss's company tends to give them a sense of security along with an opportunity to make some big money in the future. Of course, the company must be structured either as a corporation or a limited partnership to use this tact.

Companies use either of two approaches to structure such an arrangement: (1) by issuing nonvoting common shares or limited partnership units, or, (2) through an Employee Stock Ownership Plan (ESOP). Issuing nonvoting stock is a simple matter. It merely requires adding a section to the corporation's bylaws, registering new nonvoting shares in the state of incorporation, and issuing stock certificates.

Simultaneously with issuing the stock, an agreement should be executed with employees. This agreement should stipulate the various terms and conditions attached to receiving the shares.

Issuing shares of the company through an ESOP can accomplish exactly the same result as issuing nonvoting shares directly. However, the complexity of establishing an ESOP often precludes smaller companies from using this mechanism. Most ESOPs are used to raise equity capital rather than to reduce payroll costs. A brief discussion of setting up an ESOP for this purpose is included in chapter 9.

Many other possibilities exist for replacing cash payroll with noncash incentives. The choice depends on the type of business you have, the number of employees, and the type of employees. Noncash incentives as partial substitutes for wages won't always work, but enough companies have used the method that it's worth trying.

Convert Employees to Independent Contractors

Under certain conditions it is possible to operate a business entirely with independent contractors in place of employees. The advantages in doing this are obvious: you don't pay any employee benefits for independent contractors. This amounts to a significant cash savings, easily totaling 30 to 50 percent of payroll. With five employees earning average salaries of $25,000 per year, a 30 percent savings would put an additional $37,500 cash in your bank account: 50 percent would add $62,500.

An independent contractor is responsible for paying his or her own social security taxes (called self-employment taxes). A company does not withhold any taxes from the worker's paycheck, thus eliminating the need to file payroll tax returns, another cash saving. A company does not pay unemployment compensation for independent contractors either.

From an employee's perspective, the major deterrents to becoming an independent contractor are usually the loss of group health and life insurance and the loss of group pension plans. The first objection can be easily overcome by having the company subscribe to one of the many small business group health and life policies. These are specifically designed for businesses with few or no employees. Each worker can participate in the plan at his or her own expense, but at group rates significantly lower than individual coverage.

Although independent contractors cannot participate in company group pension plans, they can start their own retirement plans, both IRAs and Keogh plans. Independent contractors can also set up their own corporations and qualify for the same SEP plan previously maintained by the employer company.

As added incentive to convert employees to independent contractors, it might be necessary to compensate them for the loss of company-paid benefits. But this can be negotiated and nearly always amounts to less than the cost of employee plans.

Save Cash with Family Employees

Family members often want wages equal to or even more than outside employees. However, several cash savings accrue if you can replace existing employees with a spouse, children, or other relatives. Again, this method won't work in all companies, but especially in small retail or service businesses, family members can play an important role in recession-proofing a company. Cash savings are achieved in four ways.

1. Wages to family members might be less than wages to the replaced employee.

2. Even at the same wage, a net cash savings accrues by reducing your draw by the amount of wages drawn by family members.

3. Family members can be hired as independent contractors thus eliminating some payroll taxes.

4. Family members can continue to be covered as your dependents for group insurance purposes thus decreasing total company premium payments.

In smaller companies with one or two employees—perhaps a sales person and an office manager—qualified family members can eliminate the entire outside payroll. Recession-proofing then entails not only increasing the cash-flow of the company itself, but also the cash-flow to you. In reality, you and your company are one and the same. From this perspective, employing family member keeps company cash in the family rather than spending it outside, which is another way to improve the total cash position.

A Noncash Bonus Program

A noncash employee performance bonus program clearly cannot be counted as a cost reduction. However, it is included as a recession-proofing action because it improves cash-flow by two means.

1. Any meaningful employee bonus program should encourage increased efforts to control and reduce costs or to increase sales.

2. Noncash rewards for superior performance achieves incentive goals without a cash drain.

Chapter 4 describes a cost-effective incentive program for key management personnel that should bring in more cash than it costs. Chapter 7 illustrates how to set up a workable incentive program for sales personnel. Noncash bonus programs based on achieving specific cost reductions seem to be most effective for the rest of the company personnel.

A meaningful incentive program should exhibit seven characteristics, as shown in the following guidelines.

To be effective an employee bonus program based on cost reductions should:

1. Cover a full year of operations

2. Be broken into segments for measuring milestone achievements—month, quarter, or half year

3. Identify milestone achievement goals for each employee or group of employees

4. Have goals that are easily quantifiable

5. Reward participants at each milestone achievement as well as on cumulative annual performance

6. Have a two-part structure:

    a. One part should contain goals that can be achieved by an employee or employee group without help or interference from other departments.

    b. Another part should contain goals that must rely on other departments or employees and in this way integrate the achievements into overall company objectives.

Achievement awards should be divided into milestones (awarded as each milestone is achieved) and total program awards should be made at the end of the year for cumulative performance. The annual awards should be substantially more than those used for milestone achievements. With a cumulative effect to worry about, making each milestone becomes more relevant.

Following are a few examples of noncash awards (or those that require a small expenditure) that other companies have used effectively to motivate key employees:

1. Windbreaker jackets with company logo

2. Caps or shirts with company logo

3. Public relations announcements in employee's local newspaper

4. Prime tickets to local athletic events

5. U.S. savings bonds

6. Two extra weeks of vacation

7. Diamond lapel pins

8. Large banners with winner's name and achievement displayed in the company facility

9. With the employee's next business trip include airfare and hotel accommodations for a spouse at an

exotic vacation spot nearby (e.g., the Caribbean, Europe, New York, Los Angeles)

10. Notices sent to major customers announcing the employee's achievement

Many of these awards might not seem significant, but being recognized for a job well done often means more than the value of the reward. I have frequently found that when an owner compliments an employee publicly for superior performance that employee goes out of his or her way to do well the next time.

Conclusion

There is nothing easy about laying off loyal employees for the sake of saving cash. It takes a rare business owner who can close his or her eyes to the pain and suffering of employees who lose their only source of income. Some will find other jobs quickly. Many won't be so fortunate. During tough times, with companies slimming down and unemployment jumping, finding another position quickly becomes nearly impossible.

Laying off employees to cut costs is bound to have an impact on you as well. If laid off employees are older or lack skills currently in demand, you are, in effect, sacrificing their welfare for you own. And that hurts, badly. The last time I had to lay off over one hundred older, loyal employees to save my manufacturing company, it broke me. I know I could never do it again.

So think twice before you take the ax to people. Be sure there isn't any other way to cut the costs you need to cut. If you do decide that layoffs are the only way, be kind about it. Take the time to explain to each person individually why he or she was chosen to go rather than someone else. And then try to hire them back when things get better.

To summarize, this chapter has offered several suggestions for reducing personnel costs as part of a cost-reduction program. The effectiveness of each idea and the cash savings generated by it depend on (1) the size and type of company, (2) the number and type of employees, and (3) an owner's management style and objectives. What works in one company will probably fail in others. Some of these suggestions cost a few dollars, but sometimes it's better to spend a little to recoup a lot. In other cases it's just more money down the drain.

Creating extra cash through personnel cuts is one way to go. The next chapter takes a look at ways to reduce nonpersonnel costs in administrative areas. Chapter 7 discusses reductions in selling expenses. A meaningful cost-reduction program should encompass all areas of the business, not just one or two.

If you have been in business for several years you most likely have fine-tuned your company, balancing necessary activities and expenses between production, selling, and administrative functions. To slice costs from one area without corresponding attention to other parts of the company could easily throw this balance out of kilter, causing real harm to the business. This is definitely not the time to take that risk. Take a look at each segment and try to maintain the balance you so laboriously built up over the years.

Chapter 4

Unfixing Fixed Costs

Cutting Administrative Expenses

Fixed costs do not exist. Noncontrollable costs do not exist. Every operating expense of a going business can be controlled and varied by management prerogative. Coming from a CPA and an expert cost accountant such phrases sound like heresy. Nevertheless, from an operations perspective even costs such as depreciation, rent, property taxes, insurance, and income taxes can be controlled and therefore changed by a company's management. During tough times we're not concerned about increasing these so-called fixed costs; we are concerned about reducing them. This chapter demonstrates how it's done.

Let's dispose of the easy ones first.

Depreciation is not a cash expenditure so we don't care about reducing it. Just for the purists, however, depreciation methods and useful lives can be established by management. If you want something different than IRS guidelines, apply to the Service for an exemption. In most cases with reasonable cause it will be granted.

Lease payments for renting a building, a piece of equipment, or a vehicle appear locked in by contractual agreement. But chapter 12 discloses tips for renegotiating leases to get lower payments.

Income taxes are calculated on a company's net income. You can't do anything about the tax rate but every business owner can control the elements of sales and expenses that go into determining taxable net income. Therefore, even the amount paid for income taxes can be controlled, at least to some extent. Obviously, the timing of payments for quarterly estimated taxes can also be controlled.

So much for the easy ones. Now let's look at how to reduce the other major administrative fixed costs.

- ☐ Insurance premiums
- ☐ Real and personal property taxes
- ☐ Utilities and telephone expenses
- ☐ Freight charges
- ☐ Professional fees
- ☐ Bank charges
- ☐ Data processing costs

It goes without saying that when cost-reduction actions for each of these administrative expenses are established, they should be inserted in the cost-reduction control sheet from chapter 2. The type of budgets described in the same chapter should also be used to monitor reductions in administrative expenses.

Slice Insurance Premiums

Three types of insurance apply to most businesses: health care and perhaps life, property and product liability, and automobile. Each type should be carefully scrutinized for potential cost reductions. With group health and automobile insurance premiums going through the roof, these categories deserve the most vigorous examination, although property and liability coverage can also be reduced.

Other than not reporting claims, which defeats the whole purpose of carrying insurance, there are four ways to reduce cash expenditures for group health care premiums.

1. Change insurance underwriters.

2. Change the coverage.

3. Share the premium cost with employees.

4. Self-insure.

Even though the insurance industry remains a seller's market, the industry is as dynamic as any other. Companies continue to jockey for position. Some are merged and their operating policies change. Some employ sales promotions to enter new markets. Some shift emphasis from one type of insurance to another and promote new policy holders. Some, feeling the pinch of HMOs and aggressive promotions from the "Blues" counterattack with reduced premiums for special coverages. Nothing is fixed in the insurance industry any more than in other business. In most states, insurance companies still strive for the competitive edge.

Competitive Bids
With the exception of automobile coverage that is totally out of control and noncompetitive in some states, such as Pennsylvania and New Jersey, with a little searching most companies can come up with competitive bids to reduce premiums. The easiest and fastest way to get bids is through a good insurance agent who isn't dedicated to one or two carriers.

Unfortunately, as in many other agent-oriented businesses, large carriers have monopolized a fairly high number of independent insurance agents. However, if you can't find an unbiased agent, you can get your own quotes directly from insurance companies. Most of the smaller carriers are willing to deal direct and if pushed to the wall, a few of the large ones will also. In the health insurance segment, HMOs and the "Blues" consistently undercut other carriers. If your state-regulated Blue Cross and Blue Shield or HMO companies can substantiate broad enough geographic coverage to fit your needs, one of these is probably the way to go.

Review Coverage
If competitive bids don't come in significantly less than current premiums, the next step should be a review of coverage. On the

automotive side, do you really need $250 collision and comprehensive deductibles? Or can you manage with $1,000 each? The premium difference can be substantial. Do you really need $1 million liability coverage, or will the normal $100/$300,000 do the job? Is it really necessary to include towing reimbursements?

The one coverage I would never recommend deleting is extended coverage for rental cars. As reviewed in chapter 7, the inclusion of rental cars in company fleet coverage is a lot cheaper than paying the rental car company for it.

Property and casualty coverage should also be carefully reviewed. With insurance companies sneaking in automatic premium increases every year based on a presumed inflationary impact on replacement values, it's very possible you are paying far too much for this coverage. The likelihood of a fire or other hazard completely destroying a building, all inventory and equipment, and all company records seems remote. If it does happen, the probability that you will replace everything with spanking new assets also seems highly unlikely.

Yet much of the property coverage in place today assumes total destruction and new replacements. That's how the premium is determined. It wouldn't hurt to get an independent appraiser to take a look at your premises on the basis of replacing with used furniture and equipment and see what the result is. Chances are the values will be substantially less than your insurance covers.

Product liability coverage is fairly easy to review. Such a review can result in substantial savings. Many companies, especially in service businesses, don't bother with this coverage. Manufacturing companies should have some. The need for retailers depends on the type of merchandise sold. Professionals of course carry malpractice coverage in place of product liability. Left to an insurance carrier, a company should insure against all imaginable product damage claims. Obviously this can be carried to an extreme.

A small machine shop client manufactured aircraft parts as a third-tier subcontractor. In other words, there were two additional companies handling its parts before they ever reached an airplane. The company's insurance agent recommended aircraft liability coverage. If a plane went down, and under the very remote possibility that blame could be cast on my client's parts, this coverage would take care of it. The client had annual profits of $200,000. The annual premium for this coverage alone totaled $50,000—one-fourth of total profits. It didn't take long to recommend that my client drop this insurance completely.

Shared Premiums

Some companies use a sharing technique to cut insurance costs—at least for health care and automobile coverages. It is becoming increasingly common, especially in smaller companies, to share health care premiums with employees. If current coverage is free for the employee and a nominal amount charged for dependents, perhaps a 50-50 split would be in order. Even if an employee pays 100 percent of the premium, group policy premiums are substantially less for an employee to carry an individual policy. The same holds true for life coverage.

Chapter 7 points out how sharing automobile insurance premiums with sales personnel that have company cars is a practical way to reduce selling expenses. The same holds true with administrative personnel driving company cars. There is no reason why insurance costs shouldn't be shared, especially in tough times.

Self-Insurance

Self-insurance has become another popular way to reduce insurance costs. Formal self-insurance programs are administered by independent administrators. Less formal plans can be handled by company personnel. In either case, funding in excess of reserve limits is available to the company rather than an insurance carrier. In smaller companies with few employees, one or two company cars, and limited exposure to property damage, self-insurance for all three coverages can be very practical, and a real cash saver.

Chop Real and Personal Property Taxes

Every locale has different standards and rates for assessing both real estate and personal property taxes. Generally, however, real estate taxes are determined by applying a predetermined rate per dollar of value to an assessed valuation. Periodically, political powers change the rate to bring in more tax revenue. Occasionally, the county assessor or other political appointee makes an appraisal of the property and establishes a new assessed value.

Many smaller companies accept these reassessments as inevitable and dutifully pay their increased tax bill. You don't have to accept the assessor findings, however. You can challenge the basis for the revaluation and the factors used to compare your property with others.

In some locations, such as New York City, an entire new legal specialty has arisen to help clients dispute property assessors. Lawyers by the thousands automatically challenge property tax returns every year. The system has become so convoluted that, according to one report, more than 90 percent of the tax bills in New York City are being reduced through challenges. You may not reside in New York City, but you can still challenge the findings of your local assessor—and have a good chance of winning. In tough times you might as well try.

Personal property tax laws seem to be even more tangled than those applying to real property. Even the definition of personal property varies between states, counties, townships, and municipalities. Some assess only inventory, others only stock and bond investments. Still other assess a tax on all equipment. Some include motor vehicles. And on and on it goes.

One element seems to be common, however: the assessment occurs on a specific date each year (e.g., December 31, June 30, April 15). By knowing precisely what date applies you should be able to keep inventory at its lowest possible level on that date and also make sure other assets are as minimal as possible—even if it means moving some of them off of the premises for a while. Retailers manage this by cleaning their shelves with storewide sales in January, June, November, or whenever the date happens to hit.

People go to extremes to avoid personal property taxes. The following case illustrates how creative some can be.

A registered pharmacist, Joyce owned a pharmacy and con-venience store about 30 miles west of Philadelphia. Her store was located in a county that assessed a personal property tax on the market value of investment stocks and bonds. Joyce's store became extremely profitable as the neighborhood developed. She invested more than $500,000 in speculative stocks but kept title in her corporation.

As the market skyrocketed in value, so did her holdings. Not willing to pay what she considered an unfair personal property tax, Joyce set up a new corporation in Delaware, trans-ferred the investments from one company to another, and never filed a personal property tax return. To date she hasn't been audited, but she wonders if what she has done is legal. Not being an expert in personal property taxes, I offer no comment.

In those states taxing the assessed value of equipment as personal property, an independent appraisal of equipment values can often reduce assessed valuation. This is especially true in manufacturing businesses with substantial production facilities.

Pare Back Utilities and Telephone Expenses

The type of utility costs incurred varies substantially with the type and location of a business. Generally, however, most busi-nesses use electricity. Many use water. Some fuel. Smaller com-panies with leased space have one monthly rental covering space and utilities. Obviously there is no room to reduce utility costs in that case. When paying your own utility bills, however, a great deal can be done to save cash. Electricity seems to be the biggest utility cost for smaller businesses.

Electric Bills

All electricity comes from public utility companies. Giants ser-vice metropolitan areas, small electric companies service smaller towns, cooperatives continue in some rural areas. With state regulatory commissions establishing the rate companies can charge customers, there isn't a great deal a company can do to change the price per unit.

On the other hand, three pieces of the billing puzzle can be monitored: the number of kilowatt hours billed each month, the amount of demand hours used, and the arithmetic. All facilities using electricity have electric meters that register kilowatt hours used. The process involved in recording the hours varies from state to state, and many times from town to town. Usually the electric company sends a meter reader to record the kilowatt hours used each months. Frequently, however, customers are asked to read their own meter and send the reading to the utility. Many times estimated usage is billed monthly with an actual meter reading done periodically.

Many companies scrupulously audit supplier invoices every month to be certain they accurately reflect the quantity and description of goods or services purchased. When it comes to utility bills, however, the tendency is to pass over audit procedures in the belief that meter readings must be accurate, computer prepared bills must have the right arithmetic, and therefore errors cannot occur. WRONG!

Several things can and frequently do go wrong. Estimated quantities of kilowatt hours can be way out of line as usage varies year to year and month to month. Meter readers read the wrong hours used. The meter itself can be broken. The latter two examples occurred simultaneously at my office.

For several years I leased an office for my management consulting business. The building was an old house remodeled into four offices, each with its own electric meter. One month I noticed my electric bill shot up. For no apparent reason it was 75 percent more than the same month a year ago. The electric company blamed it on a meter reader who recorded the wrong reading and issued a revised bill.

The next month a similar disparity occurred. I checked the meter myself and verified the accuracy of the reading. The third month it happened again. By this time both the electric company and I knew something else was wrong. I requested, and then demanded, a new meter be installed. It was. The following month my bill dropped back to where it should be. Not only was the reading done incorrectly, the meter itself was broken!

Computers also make errors, especially when electric bills are based on both a constant factor and a usage factor. The demand portion remains constant and is payable monthly regardless of how much electricity is used. The usage factor, of course, is taken from the meter reading.

A manufacturing client noticed that for three continuous months its usage portion seemed inordinately high. The readings were correct so no complaint was voiced. While performing the annual audit, the company's CPA noticed the discrepancy and ran some audit tests on the bills. He found that each month the computer extension of the rate multiplied by kilowatt hours slipped a digit. Instead of $1 for example, the computer read $10! When notified, the electric company obviously issued a credit. Apparently a new, larger computer had been installed and the company was still working out the installation bugs. So computers can quite easily make mistakes.

These examples should be sufficient evidence to encourage all companies to audit their electric bills monthly; not only the kilowatt hours used but the arithmetic as well. The same goes for water, natural gas, and other utilities purchased from municipal authorities or public utilities. Water, fuel oil, coal, or natural gas purchased from private sources also bear close scrutiny. Invoices for these services should be audited monthly with the same care as invoices for supplies, materials, or legal fees.

If you haven't been paying attention to these bills, it's still possible to get refunds. Based on the three year statute of limitations, gather up all utility bills for the prior three years, whether purchased from public or private suppliers. Hire an outsider, college students are excellent and reasonably cheap sources, to check out the arithmetic and reasonableness of these bills. It shouldn't take more than a few days so the cash outlay is minimal.

It would be very surprising if you don't come up with errors. Notify the supplier and usually a refund check will be in the mail within a month. Several small businesses have found this an excellent way to raise spare cash. Once the audit process has been started, keep at it every month for current bills. You might be surprised how much you save.

Telephone Bills

Invoices for telephone service fall into the same category. Always check your phone bill each month, not only for arithmetic accuracy, but also for the propriety of long-distance charges, equipment rentals, and services. Telephone companies seem to be less accurate than other utilities.

Rural phone companies have always been subject to the same potential inaccuracies as any other small supplier, although before the AT & T breakup, major phone companies did a fairly good job. Since the formation of "baby Bells" however, and the advent of competitive long-distance service, the normal monthly phone bill looks like a catalog. And the more companies with their fingers in the telephone pie the higher the probability of billing errors.

Significant savings can frequently be generated from telephone company errors and overcharges as well as by controlling the internal use of telephones. Cost reductions in telephone expenses should begin by taking an inventory of what you currently use.

1. Take a physical inventory of all telephone equipment on the company's premises. List the bells and whistles attached to each phone—how many buttons (hold, transfer, re-dial, intercom).

2. Identify which pieces of equipment are owned by your company and which are leased from the phone company.

3. List the number of trunk lines, including private lines, coming into the company.

4. List all the phone services included with each piece of equipment and each trunk line (e.g., call waiting, call forwarding, re-dialing, conference calling).

With the inventory competed, several questions need to be answered:

1. *Do you really need all those phones scattered around the company?* Probably not. If not, sell the ones you don't absolutely need. The fewer phones, the fewer phone calls will be made. Employees are a good source of buyers for excess phone equipment. If leased, merely turn the excess phones back to the leasing company.

2. *Do you really need all those call waiting, conferencing, and other services?* Effective phone company sales pitches probably sold you on these services in the beginning, but now, when you are trying to conserve cash, does every phone need call waiting? If no, cancel the services immediately.

3. *If some phones are leased and some owned why not either buy the leased phones (at a used price of course) or sell the company-owned phones to a leasing company?* An easy cost comparison should answer which way to go.

4. *Do you really need all those trunk lines?* Most companies have more trunk lines than necessary and can easily save monthly cash by relinquishing one or more.

5. *Although dedicated trunk lines for facsimile machines and computer telecommunications are convenient, are they used enough to make them crucial to the operation?* If not get rid of the lines and use normal voice lines for fax and computers as needed. Most small companies waste money by dedicating a line to fax equipment, unless it is used continuously. Automatic answering fax machines are a convenience, not generally a necessity. The same holds true for computer telecommunications.

6. *How many times each week are 800 numbers used, both outgoing and incoming?* Although sales personnel love to have it both ways, very often an outgoing 800 number is used unnecessarily. Check with the

phone company for various alternatives—extended service for local, regional, and national calls. Run some tests for a month using and not using the 800 number for outgoing calls.

7. *Is Sprint, MCI, AT&T, or some other service the least cost for most of the calls made?* Each service has advantages. Cost advantage depends on where and how long calls are made. Don't be misled by advertising claims for any of these services.

8. *Are private trunk lines really essential?* Private lines are ego builders. As an owner you shouldn't need to boost your own ego. Private lines are an expensive toy.

9. *Can any phone be used for outgoing calls or long-distance calls?* Phone companies can restrict usage by phone station. Employee long-distance calls or personal calls are an unnecessary expense.

10. *If leasing a phone system, are you getting the best terms and the best equipment per dollar cost?* Compare the cost and quality of other systems. If a lower cost one is available with comparable or slightly less quality equipment, renegotiate out of the current lease. Many times it is less expensive to buy a phone system than to lease one. Check it out.

11. *Does your phone bill identify toll calls by phone station?* It should. If not, check with your phone company. They can rig the phones.

Two final steps can frequently reduce cash expenditures for telephones. First, be certain to keep track of toll calls—who makes them and where. Each call must be logged in by the caller. If toll calls are placed through a central switchboard or receptionist, he or she should keep the log. Every month this log should be matched to the phone bill. Refuse to pay unlogged calls. In a short time this procedure will almost certainly reduce the number of toll calls made. If it doesn't, at least you will know who to get after.

Second, audit your old phone bills. Just as with electric and other utility bills, the prior three years telephone invoices should be audited for arithmetic accuracy. The auditor should also check special charges for services and equipment to make sure you are being charged for what you have ordered and continue to need. A recent case won by the Pennsylvania Public Utility Commission and a consumer advocate group against Bell of Pennsylvania proves how important this step can be.

The Public Utility Commission (PUC) and the consumer advocate group (CAG) charged that Bell of Pennsylvania (Bell) did not clearly tell customers that inside wire maintenance plans, call waiting, call forwarding, three-way calling, and speed calling services were optional. The suit also charged that Bell gave false or misleading information about the functions of and need for certain optional services such as touch tone service. Bell was required to refund charges to customers who had any of these services between January 1, 1985, and March 20, 1988, whether or not the customer ordered them. That amounts to a sizable cash refund for companies with several phones and services.

Undoubtedly, with Bell losing this suit, other local phone companies are or will probably be forced into the same situation. Chances are, however, they will never notify customers that they are entitled to a refund. It's up to you to claim it.

Recoup Excessive Freight Payments

Freight or shipping charges can amount to a significant amount of cash outlay in the course of a year. Sometimes shipping charges sneak up on you. They are regarded as a necessary expense that must be incurred in receiving or delivering products. Some companies have their own truck fleet or use contract carriers. These shipping expenses should be reviewed in conjunction with production costs as described in chapter 2. This section is concerned with reducing common carrier shipping expense.

Common carriers may be truck lines, railroads, barges, ocean going vessels, or airplanes, any transporter of merchandise for the general public. Many service businesses do not consider shipping charges as a major expense, although many do. Consider, for example, how many times financial planners, consultants, investment advisors, literary agents, publicists, and so on ship packages through an overnight or other common carrier (e.g., Federal Express, Airborne, UPS, U.S. Express Mail). At $10 to $20 per package, it doesn't take long for these charges to add up to significant amounts.

Traditional interstate common carriers—all those except private package deliverers—base their rates on tariff schedules published for the industry and controlled by the Interstate Commerce Commission. This means that every trucker charges the same rate to transport goods direct between New York and Chicago. Every railroad charges the same between Los Angeles and Phoenix. Barges, ocean vessels, airplanes each have their own regulated set of rates.

Intrastate and intra-city shipments are different. States regulate some rates but carriers frequently compete with back-hauls, LCL loads, and intermediate drop-off points. A shipper can't gain much advantage for interstate shipping but it can obtain competitive rates for short hauls.

Reducing freight expense can be done in two ways: by getting refunds from carriers for overcharges and by the selective planning of shipments. Freight bill audit companies have been around for years. The reason is obvious: common carriers make a great many mistakes in preparing freight bills. If you have used traditional interstate common carriers over the past three years, give one of these audit firms a crack at getting you a refund.

The process is very simple. Gather up all your freight bills and ship them to a freight auditor (obviously, after executing a contract). The freight auditor checks the tariff rate on each freight bill against published tariffs. It also verifies the arithmetic calculations on the bill. Refund applications are then remitted to carriers. Refund checks are received by the audit firm which then forwards your share. Although they do vary, typically, freight audit firms keep one-third to one-half of any recovery. But they charge nothing up front. No recovery, no charge. You really can't lose.

The selective planning of shipments is just good business practice, with or without a cost-reduction program. The idea is to assign one person the responsibility for selecting the lowest cost carrier that meets the requirements of the shipper each time a shipment goes out. A package shipped from New York to Washington could go UPS, parcel post, Express Mail, by overnight carrier, bus, rail, or delivery truck.

The shipping manager compares the cost of each alternative against shipping criteria (i.e., the drop-dead time of delivery, value of merchandise, character of the package, and any other important consideration) and selects the appropriate carrier. This process takes some time and effort but in the long run is an effective way to keep shipping costs at a minimum, regardless of the type or size of business.

Trim Professional Fees

Professional fees are another one of those so-called fixed administrative costs that seem uncontrollable. Don't believe it. Professional fees can be controlled—and reduced—as easily as any other operating expense. Professional fees encompass charges from all outside professionals that you might use from time to time. Lawyers, public accountants, insurance consultants, management consultants, pension advisors, health care counselors, and so on.

Many small companies never engage pension advisors or health care counselors, but most use a lawyer or public accountant at times. The following cost-reduction recommendations apply to all professionals, not just lawyers and accountants.

One of the ways professionals get and keep clients is by cloaking their advice in indecipherable language. Lawyers talk about producing documents when they mean turning over your records. Accountants record unbilled receivables when they really mean sales you haven't had time to invoice yet. My favorite is health care language—tractionary kinesthesia for a pulled muscle.

The first step in reducing professional fees is to refuse to be boondoggled into believing you must have a lawyer or other professional on call day and night to answer routine questions.

Most of us know basic law whether we use lawyer language or not. Most of us understand that cash coming in goes in the left drawer and cash going out comes from the right drawer even though we may not understand balance sheets and income statements.

Confidence in your own ability to run a business and make reasonable business decisions coupled with access to a public library for answers to questions that stump you, will soon put you out of reach of most professionals. If you have retainer contracts with lawyers, accountants, pension advisors or other professionals tear them up. You don't need them, and they cost a bundle.

Use lawyers if you want to sue or are being sued. Use a public accountant if your bank requires an audit or you get audited by the IRS. Use a doctor if you are really sick. That's how professionals should be used, not as sounding boards. Following this rule will almost certainly reduce current expenditures for professional fees.

If you must use a professional, be absolutely certain that a contract is executed between the company and the professional. This should spell out precisely the scope of the engagement, the time involved, and the fees to be charged. Don't leave anything to chance. No loose ends.

If you don't understand some of the phrases used in the agreement, don't sign. Get them interpreted from someone. We all know we shouldn't sign anything we don't understand, yet we continue to get involved in contracts we really didn't need or want in the first place.

When you need to engage a professional get competitive bids from several who have the credentials. Professionals run businesses just like yours. Professionals compete on price, service, quality, and delivery, just like any other business. If more business people would make the effort to get competitive bids before engaging professionals, we could probably drive their fees down to reasonable levels.

Once you get the bids, interview and check references of at least three possibilities. Hiring a professional should be done with as much care as you would use when hiring an employee. Don't be afraid to question the professional's experience in the matter you need resolved. If he or she doesn't have the right experience, go on to someone else.

At first glance these suggestions appear mundane. However, each of these steps is essential to keeping professional fees down, and that's part of recession-proofing your company.

A few parting comments: be sure to tear up any retainer contract with lawyers or other professionals you might have now. Then start all over again negotiating fees and scope of service. In competitive fields such as public accounting or tax preparation, three year audit and tax preparation contracts *at a fixed price* will save money in the long run. And stay away from outside trustees for employee pension and retirement plans. There is no reason for not doing the job yourself and saving some money.

Stop Bank Charges

Bank charges are another category of administrative expense that seem to be noncontrollable. If the bank says it charges $30 for an overdraft check, they merely deduct it from the account. The same with monthly service fees, charges for check printing, statement maintenance fees, and a variety of other charges.

Banks get away with these usurious charges because customers feel locked into a specific bank and hardly ever get bids from competing banks. Yes, banks do compete. At times it's hard to see the competition, but it's there nonetheless.

Contrary to what banker's would like us to believe, just because we have a loan from a bank does not mean we must conduct all our banking with the same bank. A bank might require that a certain balance be kept on deposit as a condition of granting the loan. That's all right. All other cash could go to a more competitive bank, however. One that charges less and therefore conserves your cash.

Because bank policies keep changing with the wind, it's necessary to keep a close watch not only on what your bank is charging, but also on policies of other banks in your area. If someone else offers better rates or charges lower fees, move your checking or saving account. If the original bank comes in line eventually you can always move everything back again.

Just be careful you don't get soaked twice for printing new checks.

One way to avoid this is to maintain very small checking balances in several banks and use the one offering the lowest rates and fees. Then you can switch back and forth without printing new checks. I used this tactic when I ran a small-business accounting practice. I maintained the minimum balance in four different banks—just enough to avoid monthly charges. As one or the other changed its policies, I merely transferred my checking funds to the new bank.

Don't let banks fool you into believing that you can't get a better deal elsewhere. There is usually at least one bank in your area that will charge you less than the one you are using, at least for a while. And every little bit helps in tough times.

Curtail Computer Costs

The final major cost-reduction area of administrative expenses relates to computer (or data processing) activities. Many companies have been led to believe that a computer will replace personnel and therefore is an excellent tool for reducing labor costs. Not so. Over and over again, companies that have installed computers find that the number of salaried personnel actually increases. In addition, several nonpersonnel expenses accompany computers, as anyone who has been involved in a computer installation knows. So the first tip about computers is don't get one as a cost-reduction step.

For companies already blessed with a computer installation, whether personal computers or a full-fledged computer mainframe, several cost-reduction actions might be appropriate.

1. Move your payroll to a service bureau. Either a national service bureau such as Automatic Data Processing (ADP) or most local banks can calculate payroll, write payroll checks, and summarize information for payroll tax returns, for substantially less cost than doing it in-house.

2. Take personal computers away from everyone who doesn't use one frequently. Personal computers (PCs) have become a status symbol in many companies. Everyone must have one on his or her desk. If it isn't crucial to the performance of a job, get rid of it. Less time will be wasted and fewer office supplies used.

3. Take an inventory of what applications are used on computers now. A mainframe with just payroll and accounts receivable is underutilized. Get rid of it and use some of the proceeds to buy one or two small PCs. Does your secretary really need a powerful 40 megabyte hard drive PC? If a smaller model will suffice, downgrading will save time and supplies. Conversely, if complicated calculations must be made on a low-capacity model, substantial time and money can be saved by upgrading to a bigger model (a used one of course).

4. Take advantage of free computer training courses. At least one computer store in your area probably offers free training. Don't pay for it if you don't have to.

5. Buy only those computer supplies you need for the next month. Computer paper and ribbons are expensive. If you can't get a substantial volume discount, buy only what you need.

6. Stay away from PC maintenance contracts. These machines seldom break down and if they do, the cost of repairing them is usually less than annual maintenance contracts. The exception is laser printers, which are very fragile.

7. Inventory your software programs. Some software developers offer annual upgrades at very low prices (under $100). But don't fall for the sales

pitch that every upgrade is better than last year's model.

Larger companies with computer mainframes and a full complement of data processing personnel find many more cost-reduction actions without damaging the efficiency of the service. Data processing departments are notorious for becoming fat overnight. If you have one, you can almost arbitrarily cut 10 to 15 percent off data processing costs simply by telling your manager to do it.

Install a Key Management Incentive Program

Before leaving the administrative area, a program to motivate administrative managers to reduce costs and keep them down should be considered. It doesn't make any difference whether you have one employee or 100 employees, as discussed several times already, someone must be assigned the responsibility of implementing cost reductions.

Although you must assume ultimate responsibility and exercise your prerogative for final decision making, someone else in the company should actually do the legwork. If the one employee is a secretary or a salesperson, the choice becomes obvious. Companies with several employees should assign responsibility to those individuals with the authority to make the specific cost reductions happen.

On the dark side, managing a cost-reduction program is seldom any fun. It's hard work. It requires laying people off, and that nearly always hurts. Implementing many of the action steps can be messy, especially when dealing with suppliers or outside professionals. Managing cost reductions is never an enjoyable experience.

Anyone assigned to manage cost reductions should be given a serious incentive to perform effectively—other than keeping his or her job. So along with reducing cash expenditures, it's entirely possible that a key manager incentive program will have to be implemented even if it costs a few dollars.

The keys to an effective management incentive program for both administrative and sales personnel (see chapter 7) are

☐ Performance goals that can be controlled by the individual

☐ Methods to measure results against these goals

☐ An achievement award that is meaningful to the recipient

It's human nature to want to be rewarded for a job well done. Whether a secretary in a very small business, the president of a giant corporation, or any employee in between, a promised reward for superior performance inevitably motivates a person beyond normal achievement levels. And that's what you need to make a cost reduction program work—achievement beyond normal levels.

Begin by sitting down with whomever you chose to run the show and be certain he or she understands what cost-reduction actions must be taken, when they should occur, and what results you expect. This person should also be intimately involved in preparing the cost reduction layout schedule described in chapter 2.

If the program stretches beyond twelve months, achievement milestones should be set at least quarterly. In this case, the ultimate reward should be parceled out each quarter, as earned, with the bulk of it reserved for cumulative performance over twelve months. A program extending into a second year, or more, should command a new incentive program each twelve months. No one wants to wait forever for a reward.

The cost-reduction program itself, if properly structured, will indicate the expected results from each action and the timing of these results. This then becomes the standard against which to measure the individual's performance.

Finally, before implementation begins, work out the type of award each key manager will receive. This becomes the key to any effective incentive program. If an employee needs cash, then cash awards should be made—significant enough to make all the effort worth while. Fifty percent of annual salary is a good starting point. Perhaps the employee would rather have time off. A month to six weeks with pay should work. Or maybe the employee values vacations. How about an expense-paid trip to the Caribbean for a month?

Regardless of the specific award, be sure the employee really values it, and that it is significant enough to make a real difference in the employee's life. As so often happens in companies large and small, an incentive program that scrimps on the amount of the award or grants something that the employee isn't very excited about never motivates as it was intended. Get the cash-flow from cost reductions. Pay some of it back for superior performance.

Improving cash-flow is never an easy task. In tough times it becomes doubly difficult. Yet, improving cash-flow is the cornerstone of any effective recession-proofing program. These first chapters have set out proven methods for improving cash-flow by reducing costs. The next three chapters look at the flip side of the equation—improving cash-flow through marketing and sales strategies. Combining cost reductions with marketing and sales strategies, a company should be in an excellent position to weather the storm of economic turmoil.

Chapter 5

Protective Marketing

Strategies for a Recession-Proof Market Position

Protective marketing means optimizing prices, volume, and margin while minimizing expenditures for selling expenses. Stated another way, recession-proof sales tactics call for selling the greatest quantity of product or services with the highest gross margins while spending the least amount on advertising, sales promotions, public relations, sales salaries, and other selling expenses.

Market control is the key to protective marketing. With control of your markets you can manage pricing, deliveries, packaging, new product introductions, and customer service policies; control inventory levels and returned goods; and maximize cash collections. Market control leads to the optimization of sales turnover, which in turn allows the most efficient use of selling tools to keep cash expenditures at the lowest possible level.

Market control is achieved by actions taken in one or a combination of three conditions: optimum product mix, managed customer mix, and cost-effective after-sale service.

Optimizing product mix means the selective selling of products with the optimum matching of sales volume and product margin.

Managing customer mix means identifying and concentrating on customers willing and able to pay the highest price for the quality and quantity of products that can be produced most efficiently.

Cost-effective after-sale service ensures repeat sales of the right products to the right customers.

Market control is an effective method for growing a company in boom times. It also serves as the least risk, highest results strategy for recession-proofing a company in tough times. Market control strategies coupled with cost-effective selling tactics always yield the optimum profits for any company.

This chapter examines alternative product-customer-market strategies to achieve market control and corollary ways to decrease cost or increase sales dollars. The next chapter recommends cost-effective advertising and public relations strategies that can assist in this effort. Chapter 7 looks at ideas and methods for minimizing cash expenditures for selling expenses and monitoring planned sales strategies. If you are already experiencing a severely shrinking product demand or customer base, take a look at chapter 11 for some ideas about opening new markets.

The starting point in achieving market control is to define specifically what markets you currently serve. Most markets can be defined geographically (e.g., a neighborhood, a city, a region, a nation, or more), by type of customer (e.g., upscale, budget, prime contractors, chain stores), by pricing strategy (e.g., high, mid-range, low), quality standards (e.g., high quality, throw aways), or product specifications (e.g., standard shelf products, made-to-order products).

A cardinal rule in protective marketing is that a supplier cannot afford to be all things to all customers. You must identify what specific market niches you want to go after and then structure a marketing strategy to control those markets. Companies that define a marketing strategy to penetrate a wide range of markets generally end up unable to control pricing, quality standards, distribution channels, or customer service in any of them. Margins are always higher when you control a market than when you are merely one of many followers.

Shift Product Mix
The term *product* doesn't necessarily refer to something you can feel and touch. Service businesses also sell products—products

that happen to be in the form of services. The term *product mix* refers to both types of products—the touch and feel type and the service variety.

Varying product mix can be a strategically effective weapon to gain market share from competitors, for improving margins, and to raise cash. In most cases recession-proofing actions to modify product mix result in all three benefits. The least understood, however, is how changing the product mix can actually increase market share. In effect, variations in product mix can put a company in greater control of its market.

Increase Market Share
Most companies sell more than one product. Obviously retail stores do. Manufacturing firms usually produce at least three or four different products and most often many more. Service businesses generally offer a variety of products each priced differently.

The proportionate mix of each product or product line sold to a given market is frequently left to market demand. If latex paint is a big seller but oil-based mixes trail, quite naturally a paint store will stock more latex than oil-based paints. If the store carries brands from several latex paint manufacturers, customers choose a brand based on sales promotions, advertising, price, reputation, and availability of colors. Market share remains fairly constant, controlled primarily by perceived standards, price, and special promotions.

On the other hand, assume a manufacturer promotes an oil-based paint providing easy cleanup, better coverage, broader color choices, and greater longevity than latex brands, even though these characteristics exist in its current line. The paint is priced higher than existing oil-based and latex choices. Further assume that the manufacturer elects to target the modified product to upscale retail buyers.

Providing the proper sales pitch is used, it's entirely possible that the oil-based line will begin outselling latex, and therefore change proportionate market shares. Unless the oil-based line fails to perform as promoted, the manufacture has exerted market control and improved its profit margins simply by changing its product mix strategy.

Another method for increasing market share by shifting product mix can be accomplished through product pruning. In many companies a general rule of thumb states that 20 percent of the products account for 80 percent of the profits. Although perhaps not universally applicable to companies offering three of four products, it does generally hold for those with more. Over time, businesses tend to add products as market conditions change but seldom delete a product from the line unless it becomes totally obsolete. This is especially true in retail and manufacturing companies, but applies in service businesses as well.

By pruning out the 80 percent of a company's products that account for 20 percent of the profits, several benefits accrue. Two relate to increasing market share, two improve margins, and a fifth directly increases cash-flow.

Market share is increased on the front end of the sale by decreasing prices below competitor's levels, and on the back end by improving customer service. Price reductions for the remaining 20 percent of the products can occur without hurting margins because the cost of producing these products goes down. As described in the next section of this chapter, this happens because part of the product pruning process involves internal cost reductions (e.g., personnel layoffs, reduced materials and supplies, lower telephone and utilities costs, and so on).

These cost reductions invariably create greater efficiency and productivity in producing the remaining products, which in turn reduces their production costs. By sharing these reduced costs with customers through decreased prices, a company usually gains at least a temporary market advantage.

This temporary advantage can often turn into a permanent increased market share by following price reductions with improved customer service. The same types of cost reductions resulting from deleting noncritical products allow customer service personnel to spend more time and greater effort servicing sales from the remaining products.

Improved Product Margins

Even with price reductions for remaining products, product pruning improves overall margins by two additional means. The first relates to reductions in overall personnel. Chapter 3 pointed out how significant cash savings are realized by reducing payroll and associated benefits. Reductions in direct production personnel improve product margins. Reductions in overhead personnel affect the overall profitability of the company.

When products are pruned, total sales usually fall. This can be a frightening occurrence but should not have an adverse impact on profitability or cash-flow. On the contrary, if the deleted products were not adding substantially to the total profit of the company it means the cost of producing them was nearly equal to or greater than the sale realized. Therefore, a reduction in sales corresponding to reduced costs won't adversely affect cash-flow at all.

As nonproductive overhead drops, the only impact on profits can be an improvement. Margins improve not only because fewer people are on the payroll, but also because non-payroll costs normally vary to a large extent with the number of people employed. Fewer people use fewer supplies, make fewer telephone calls, and require less electricity. Reductions in all of these areas improves product margins.

Intentionally shrinking a product offering also reduces the amount of purchased materials and supplies. Not only does this save cash, it also permits purchasing personnel to concentrate more fully on buying materials needed to produce the products left intact. Such concentrated efforts to search out new suppliers offering lower prices, better terms, or more effective delivery times frequently results in improved margins.

Companies selling high material content products reap the greatest benefits. Service and retail businesses realize less improvement by more efficient purchasing efforts but usually save some amounts through the prudent selection of suppliers.

Although the primary purpose in product pruning is to improve the market position of the remaining products while simultaneously reducing operating costs, selling off obsolete assets is a terrific way to create extra cash-flow as a byproduct of the action. Whether sold individually or as a spin-off, assets dedicated to products no longer sold should be disposed of as soon as possible. Improved efficiency and productivity of personnel is another byproduct of the action. Although difficult (if not impossible) to measure, positive effects on personnel almost always occur after serious product pruning.

Raise Cash

The final benefit from pruning marginally profitable or unprofitable products comes from selling unneeded business assets. Specific machinery, vehicles, office equipment, or other hard assets used to produce, store, or deliver products deleted from the line should be sold. If separate space is used to house this equipment it can also be sold, sublet, or returned to the lessor. Materials on hand that are used to produce the deleted products can be sold or returned to suppliers for credit or refunds.

Larger companies that actually segregate product groupings in separate facilities or divisions often decide to sell the entire facility as a unit rather than dispose of each asset piecemeal. Groups of employees operating this division or facility are excellent candidates as buyers.

Manage Customer Mix

One of the most successful marketers I have ever met preached that managing customer mix was the best way to improve market control. His favorite saying was, "concentrate your selling efforts on smart customers and let the dumb ones go." Over the years I have learned that a selective customer mix can do as much or more to gain control of a market than any other single action. And it applies to virtually any type of business or market. Two cases illustrate how the principle works in different types of businesses.

> Bob employed three sales people in his furniture store. His top salesman, who had over thirty years experience selling high-end furniture, had a heart attack four months earlier. Sales of

high-end styles were slipping badly while sales of low-end pieces remained about constant.

Bob noticed his three sales people seemed to concentrate on those customers who didn't know specifically what they wanted and steered them to the low-end merchandise trying to boost volume. Customers who did know what they wanted became disillusioned with this tactic and often left the store without buying anything.

Bob directed one of his sales people to handle only knowledgeable customers and pass the others on to the other two sales people. In six months sales of high-end furniture substantially increased while sales of low-end pieces remained constant.

In another case,

Brad Snofel ran an auto repair shop and took the time to explain to customers exactly what caused their car to break down and how they might avoid such repairs in the future. He had more business than he could handle even though his prices were significantly higher than those charged by his friend John Olsen who had a shop across the street.

John's business fell off substantially during the last recession. Frustrated, he asked Brad to explain his secret. Obligingly, Brad explained how educating his customers turned them into smart buyers who were willing to pay higher prices because they understood exactly why their cars broke down and what Brad did to repair them. This gave them confidence that he wasn't ripping them off.

Selling to smart customers nearly always increases market share. Most smart buyers are willing to pay for quality products and services. Customer loyalty is easier to establish with smart customers. Delivery aggravations tend to disappear when a smart buyer understands why the truck didn't arrive on time. And repeat business is much easier to attain with smart buyers. These factors add up to market control and therefore increased market share.

Managing customer mix can also be accomplished by eliminating certain types of buyers. One of the objectives in managing customer mix is to concentrate on those customers who generate the highest margin per product sold. Margins are not determined by price alone, although certainly price is a major influence. The costs of convincing the customer to buy your products, the expenses of getting the product to the customer, presale storage expenses, sales commissions, and other selling expenses all come off a product's selling price and therefore reduce margins.

For example, assume a company sells hand tools to three classes of customer: discount retail chains, privately owned hardware stores, and manufacturing companies. The cost of producing the product is identical for each class of customer. Manufacturing companies are willing to pay the highest price because they like the quality of the tools, although this class also accounts for the lowest volume.

Hardware stores buy a greater volume, but aren't as concerned about the high quality so they want to pay a lesser price. Discount chains are mainly concerned with volume. They buy large quantities but demand a much lower price.

Let's further assume that a company must employ four salespersons to cover discount chains, two to handle hardware sales, and that all manufacturing sales are house accounts. Also, manufacturing customers willingly pick up from the factory, hardware stores want door-to-door delivery, and chains will only buy through regional distributors.

To maximize margins, the company must compare not only sales volume from each customer class, but associated selling costs as well. In this example, the costs of getting the product into the hands of the chain stores tripled that of selling to manufacturers and was one and one-half as expensive as selling to hardware stores. As a recession-proofing strategy, this company would be far better off taking lower sales volume and higher margins from manufacturers than selling to chain stores.

Although the age-old sales argument that you must have volume to cover overhead has a ring of truth, well-managed companies often find that careful internal cost controls allow them to pick and choose the highest margin customer to concentrate on. Volume alone without corresponding margin improvements seldom contributes significantly to increased cash-flow, assuming of course that you sell to markets where customer mix can actually be managed. As we all know, in some markets that's impossible.

Other facets of customer mix should also enter the equation. Are you better off on the production side by selling to customers willing to buy long production runs of products rather than short runs? Can you improve margins by concentrating on customers who demand high quality products that may cost more to produce but sell at higher prices, or just the reverse (the Cadillac versus Ford comparison)? Will contracting or expanding your geographic customer base yield more profits?

The answer to any or all of these questions affects the most desirable customer mix depending on the type of business you have. However, regardless of which specific areas have the greatest impact on your company, focusing on the management of customer mix provides another sound tool for developing protective marketing strategies.

Improve After-Sale Customer Service
In nearly every company regardless of size or type of business, competitive pressures are forcing increased emphasis on after-sale customer service. In most businesses, efficient after-sale service stimulates customer loyalty and repeat business and therefore should be a cornerstone of any protective marketing strategy. Sears and General Electric have both proven time and again how attention to customer service increases sales from previous customers and new customers alike. Generally, the smaller the company the more important after-sale service becomes.

After-sale service takes many forms, depending on the type of business. You might need an 800 number for customers to get technical information or instructions about the product. Perhaps a no-questions-asked returned goods policy is appropriate. Some companies find that free or low-priced instructional or repair service at the customers location gives them a competitive edge. Others offer free delivery, advance notice of sales promotions, telephone ordering, or customer training.

Regardless of the type of service offered, a sound protective marketing strategy should include more or better after-sale services than competitors offer. This usually low-cost effort can do as much or more to position a company as a market leader than practically any other policy. Some businesses have come up with innovative gimmicks for after-sale service that quickly set them apart from competition. One such example occurred in the vinyl siding business.

> The owner of Okept Roofing and Siding Company decided he needed to come up with a sales gimmick to compete with several larger firms moving into his market. Conducting a poll of previous customers, he learned that their biggest complaint was the discoloration of siding created by soot and other particles emitted from a nearby factory.
>
> Vinyl siding lasts for years so no repeat business is likely. Therefore, competitors saw no reason to offer any after-sale service. The owner of Okept saw his opening. He mailed circulars to customers from the past five years offering to power-hose their siding as a promotion service. He also stated that additional wash jobs would cost a mere $50 each. Eighty percent of his customers accepted his one-time promotion offer and of these, 60 percent signed up for the annual contract. He not only created a new market but his attention to service strengthened Okept's reputation in the area. As a result, Okept continued to beat out competition for the next five years.

Selective market penetration, varying product mix, managing customer mix, and after-sale customer service are all effective protective marketing strategies aimed at increasing market control. They won't all work with equal effectiveness for all companies. However, they all merit serious consideration for improving your cash-flow position, especially during tough times.

Other tactics are also important in the race to improve your cash position. One possibility is to combine costly market research and service activities with other companies. Joint ventures are a handy mechanism to accomplish this.

Shared Market Research
Market research can be an expensive undertaking for many businesses. Too often companies that desperately need to engage in market research activities to explore developing new

markets or to understand what is happening to their existing markets shy away from the endeavor because of cost.

At the very time new research should be conducted to cope with changing product technology, distribution techniques, and customer demand, small businesses by the hundreds seem to be content to follow the leader, to let their competition set the pace. Cost reduction programs to increase cash-flow frequently take precedent over ways to accomplish the same end through new or expanding markets.

There just isn't any room left in the budget for market research. Cash for investigative travel, subscriptions to market and product trend data, and market testing campaigns must be used for production payroll or material purchases. When cash gets tight, a natural reaction for many business owners is to delay spending on market research until conditions improve. Unfortunately, time and again this has proven to be false economy. While one company waits out tough times, competitors jump in to take a larger market share.

There are three readily available solutions to this dilemma. Many trade associations, especially those in industries characterized by many small firms, do a reasonably good job of compiling market data in their computer databases. For a minimum charge, member companies can either get printouts or direct computer-to-computer transfer of market-customer-product trends, composite ratios, trade statistics, and a variety of other information about their specific industry.

One drawback to using trade association data, however, is that the same information is available to all members. Therefore, your competitors have access to the same market information you do and the intelligence edge is lost.

Several federal and state agencies also maintain industry and market statistics in computerized databases. Agencies of the U.S. Department of Commerce have developed an international system to accumulate market, product, and customer data through their broad-reaching Computer Information Management System (CIMS). Contact your local Department of Commerce office for a listing of the reports you can get and the cost.

A third, and probably the most effective way to keep the cost of market research down is by forming a joint venture arrangement with other companies. Instead of each company incurring expense to accumulate the same data, joining forces with competitors, customers, or other companies to share both cost and information can keep cash expenditures to a minimum.

If your markets are broad enough, sharing information with a few competitors may not be too harmful. On the other hand, if your market is local, or restricted, or if there are only two or three competitors in the market, sharing research data can be deadly. So whether this is a viable alternative depends entirely on your specific market situation.

Sharing the expense of providing customer service activities might also work under the right circumstances. This gets a bit trickier to administer but if set up properly can be an extremely effective cost-saving device. It tends to work best with very small businesses without employees (or at most with one or two clerical employees). Examples could include bookkeeping and tax services, health care businesses, delivery and trucking firms, taxi companies, management consultants, distributors, contractors, single store retailers, travel agencies, and so on.

After-sale services in these examples normally involve telephone responses to customer inquires or customer complaints. A single office can be set up and staffed by one or more telephone answering people. Standard responses to complaints or queries can be written down by each business owner and placed near the telephone operator for easy access.

As calls come in, sympathetic listening and courteous responses suffice in many instances. Those callers who are not satisfied can easily be transferred to the appropriate business phone. If the business office isn't staffed, the service person merely takes the callers number and notifies the business owner to return the call in the evening or the next day.

Although shared customer service facilities are not as effective as in-house customer service departments, many small firms can't afford the latter and shared service does address the problem at least in part. If you go this route, be sure to structure the shared service facility to be dedicated to customer service. Don't let it become a telephone answering service. Contracting for a telephone answering service is relatively inexpensive. It makes no sense to divert customer service resources to answer the phone.

Increase Product Offering

Increasing the number of products or services offered for sale is another way to boost sales volume during tough times. Very few smaller companies have enough cash or talent to engage in full-scale product development programs, which can easily run into six figures. This, plus the cash required for market testing prior to introducing a new product or product line, often exceeds a company's capabilities.

On top of these development costs, perhaps an expanded sales force is required to handle the new lines, or additional delivery capabilities, variations in customer service procedures, or enhanced product testing equipment and procedures. When added together, the cash required to bring a totally new product through development, market testing, and customer acceptance stages can be enormous, usually far in excess of a small company's cash constraints. Subcontracting a new line of products or services avoids these costs.

Small manufacturing companies have used subcontracting for years to add incremental sales without incurring development costs. Some have found this route so lucrative that they have phased out their own product lines and gone exclusively to subcontracting. Small metal working or assembly operations are especially adaptable, as Zit-Flo Corp. proved.

> Zit-Flo Corp. assembled and tested a line of residential water filtration systems. The company employed four assemblers, two test engineers, and a sales manager. Another local firm selling to the military booked an order calling for monthly deliveries of rifle trigger mechanisms. The order extended over a three-year period. Additional orders absorbed shop capacity and the company subcontracted the assembly of the triggers to Zit-Flo.
>
> By adding one additional assembler and one inspector, Zit-Flo added $500,000 a year to its sales base. Today, Zit-Flo has expanded its subcontracting business to other government

contractors. This business now accounts for more than 50 percent of total sales.

Service businesses are less prone to try this method. When properly structured however, subcontracting can work as well here as with manufacturing firms. Testing labs are a good example. With equipment and personnel already in place to test various characteristics of product materials for aerospace or military products, a company should be able to easily adapt procedures to perform similar testing for the Federal Aviation Administration or even the Environmental Protection Agency.

In another type of service business,

> Clarice found subcontracting to be an excellent way to increase billings in her small public accounting firm without adding one dollar of cost. Clarice specialized in audits and reviews for state and federal compliance reporting for brokerage houses, security dealers, and investment advisors. This year-round market seldom experienced seasonal cycles. As her practice grew, Clarice added a few personnel to handle the preparation of individual tax returns. The tax side of her business didn't expand as expected and several employees had time on their hands.
>
> Through her professional contacts Clarice arranged to review tax returns prepared by two other CPA firms with expanding tax practices. These firms prepared the returns and delivered them to Clarice. Her staff referenced the returns, checked them for mathematical accuracy, and then returned them to the preparing firm. Over the course of a year, this subcontracting work added another 15 percent to Clarice's billings, without adding one dollar of extra cost.

If subcontracting seems like a viable alternative, a few simple rules should be followed.

Ten Rules Of Subcontracting

Do

1. Solicit subcontracting work from companies in similar businesses.

2. Take on jobs requiring similar quality standards.

3. Insist on advance payment or COD terms—carrying receivables is an added cost.

4. Use subcontracting as fill-in work.

5. Insist that subcontract customers furnish all materials and supplies required to do the job.

Don't

1. Take on subcontracting jobs requiring additional administrative or sales personnel.

2. Accept work that will add significantly to nonpersonnel costs (electricity, water, space).

3. Subcontract projects that increase hazardous risk costs (liability insurance, worker's compensation, health insurance claims).

4. Take jobs that might cause pollution or safety hazards in violation of government regulations.

5. Perform work for competitors.

Conclusion

This chapter has reviewed a number of protective marketing strategies that can be implemented as part of a recession-proofing process. The emphasis has been placed on controlling markets. With market control, a company can influence prices, deliveries, packaging, quality standards, and customer service. It can maximize the effect of selling policies. It can materially improve product margins. The greater the degree of control a company has over its markets the more likely it is to survive tough times.

The primary determinant of market control is how big a share a company achieves in a given market. The starting point is to clearly define your markets (geographically, by type of customers, by pricing strategy, by quality standards, or by product specifications).

Once you understand the specific market niches you sell into, protective marketing steps can be implemented to achieve control. These broad steps were identified as:

☐ varying product mix

☐ managing customer mix

☐ creative after-sales customer service

In addition to taking actions to gain market control, you can improve cash-flow by reducing the cost of market research activities. This can be accomplished in some industries by using data collected by trade associations or government agencies. In other industries, joint ventures set up between two or more companies to conduct market research share the expense. Similar cost-saving techniques can be used for after-sale customer service functions.

Cash-flow can also be improved by generating extra sales without a corresponding increase in materials, supplies, or selling expenses. Subcontracting work from other companies with similar products, processes, and quality standards is one way many companies achieve this objective.

With protective marketing strategies in place you should be ready to examine cost-effective advertising and public relations tactics to use in implementing them. You should also begin looking at ways to reduce selling expenses and methods for increasing sales volume. The next two chapters cover these areas.

Chapter 6

Spreading The Word

Cost-Effective Advertising and Public Relations

When times get tough it is tempting to treat advertising and public relations as less critical than production or selling. Before taking a slice out of production or selling payrolls, it seems much easier to reduce or even eliminate new sales brochures, stop public relations programs, or scrimp on media advertising. While there may be justification for such tactics—advertising expenditures do tend to get out of hand during boom times—both advertising and public relations are usually crucial to improving market control and therefore to generating additional cash-flow. The trick is to develop programs that are cost-effective; to implement advertising and public relations methods that produce the biggest bang for the buck.

Properly structured, advertising can be an effective tool in protective marketing. Misused, it drains cash and returns nothing. Effective advertising serves three purposes.

- ☐ It brings in new customers to the market.

- ☐ It captures customers from competitors.

- ☐ It provides market intelligence.

When coupled with a well-conceived public relations program, advertising dollars may well be the best and most cost-effective way to gain control of markets.

A cost-effective advertising campaign consists of four parts.

1. Matching the types of advertising with specific protective marketing objectives.

2. Developing creative campaigns that achieve the greatest market impact.

3. Identifying the market effect of specific advertising tactics.

4. Keeping the expenses of implementing advertising programs to a minimum.

The following sections explore tactics to achieve each of these objectives.

Match Advertising with Protective Marketing Objectives
Chapter 5 described two primary protective marketing objectives:

☐ to identify and control specific market niches, and,

☐ to keep market research and after-sale customer service expenses to a minimum.

Advertising plays a major role in achieving both objectives.

Whether the objective is to bring in new customers to the market or to usurp market share from existing competitors, advertising probably provides market intelligence and creates customer demand faster and with less cash outlay than any other means. In many cases, selective, low-key advertising is often the only feasible way to test new markets prior to entry.

One of the most effective techniques for bringing in new customers, whether new to the market or buying from competitors, uses clip-out return forms for obtaining more product information. A high number of returns indicates potential for making a major impact on the market. The reverse generally indicates trying something else.

Clip-out coupons can be a cost-effective method for stealing customers from competitors. The coupon is designed to stimulate customer interest in your company's product as opposed to a competitor's. Comparisons of price, delivery, and quality are common. The accent is on selling a product rather than on gaining market information.

Advertising agencies use a variety of methods to get the clip-out form to the market. Direct mailings with return post cards, newspaper and magazine advertisements with a cut-out form, television spot commercials with an 800 phone number, trade shows and convention booths with mail-back handouts and customer registration are a few examples.

The cost of each method varies substantially. Choosing one over the other depends on the type of product, size of the market, competitive advertising, and the role customer information requests play in a company's overall marketing strategy. Which brings us to the most critical decision point in developing a cost-effective advertising campaign—establishing short- and long-term objectives.

Business owners frequently become disillusioned with advertising because they don't see immediate results. Others change agencies because competition seems to be beating them in the marketplace. Still others stop advertising completely during tough times because it is an easy expense to eliminate. Most advertising campaigns fail to deliver expected results for one of two reasons: the expected results are not defined ahead of time or the campaign is too short to get results.

Without a carefully defined, results-oriented, self-managed program, advertising expenditures nearly always exceed original plans and the results are nearly always disappointing. Specific expected results must be quantified. How many responses to a clip-out campaign? How much sales increase of a specific product? How many new customers? What market share increase?

Most of these results cannot be achieved in the short-run, regardless of how good the advertising campaign is structured and managed. One week, one month, even six months may be too short a period to realize concrete benefits. The protective marketing strategies outlined in Chapter 5 take time to implement. So do advertising results.

Don't fall for the pitch that the more you spend on advertising the more customers you will take from competition. This hardly ever works. Unless customers realize continued, long-term benefits from switching brands or companies any gain through advertising will be short lived.

Strategically, advertising techniques to increase market share from competition should be viewed as a long-term investment. Permanent increases in market share are almost impossible to measure over the short term, unless of course your product life is short—say one year—and industry cycles are short, such as in the retail toy business. In this case, *permanent* may mean one Christmas season, one summer, or one ski season. In any event, to achieve cost-effectiveness in an advertising campaign, the specific advertising program must be matched with specific objectives in a given market.

It is often difficult to judge how much to spend on advertising and what type of media to use. In boom times, when you are turning substantial profits and your cash drawer is overflowing, it's tempting to go with the advice of your advertising agency. That's all right, if you can afford it. But experience has shown that left to their own devices advertising agencies, large and small, believe that the more you spend and the greater the variety of media, the more effective the campaign. As we all know, this hardly ever works.

The basic rule for making advertising cost effective is to develop a comprehensive program that meets your needs but no more. In other words, use only as much advertising as you really need to control your markets or to capture specific new markets. The following ten guidelines provide a helpful reference point.

Guidelines For Protective Marketing Advertising

1. Use advertising to achieve specific purposes (e.g., to test new markets, increase a specific market share, gather intelligence about new markets), not for public image building.

2. Define precise, quantifiable objectives expected from each advertising campaign, such as the anticipated number of replies to clip-outs or the number of new customers obtained.

3. Design advertising programs to target specific protective marketing goals, such as raising prices by 5 percent or increasing sales volume by 10 percent in a given market.

4. Manage the advertising campaign yourself. Don't turn control over to an advertising agency.

5. Define targeted recipients before starting the advertising campaign (i.e., types of customers, geographic coverage, specific competitors).

6. If targeting a campaign to take business from competition, know who your competition is and use product or brand names.

7. Define the time frame within which results are expected.

8. Segregate short-term expectations from long-term objectives, and use different advertising techniques for each.

9. Establish a schedule for the advertising agency to follow, including progress milestones that can be measured.

10. Devise a follow-up procedure to monitor the advertising agency against the schedule.

Achieve the Greatest Market Impact

When asked what media has the greatest market impact, most advertising executives are quick to point to television spots on highly rated, prime time programs. Coincidentally, this happens to be one of the most expensive ways to get your message across. For most companies it is anything but cost effective. The choice of advertising media seems unlimited. Every year Madison Avenue comes up with new methods for selling advertising. For smaller businesses, however, one or more of the following fifteen choices seem to work best, although not necessarily in the order listed. What is best for you depends on the specific company and product line.

1. Product and company brochures

2. Direct mailings to existing customers

3. Direct mailings to potential new customers

4. Newspaper announcements

5. Popular magazine and trade journal ads

6. Billboards or posters—roadside or indoor (e.g., at a sports arena)

7. Television spots—network or local

8. Commercial envelope flyleaves

9. Matchbooks

10. Holiday cards

11. Pencils, pens

12. Calendars

13. Newsletters

14. Telephone yellow pages

15. Catalogs

Although media cost is important, the audience is more crucial. If you are trying to sell in England, advertising in American telephone directories won't help, but newspaper announcements in the *London Times* might work well. If you have a financial planning or tax return business serving a local market it doesn't do any good to advertise on network television. However, a local channel might be just the ticket, as Maureen learned in a hurry.

> Maureen was a certified financial planner just beginning her own business. After getting only two clients in six months she decided to spend some money on advertising. Her close friend dared her to invest in a thirty-second spot commercial on a local TV channel. She purchased ten spots over a two-week period.
>
> Trying to cut corners, Maureen devised her own ad. She stood in front of the camera, told the audience what services she performed, announced that the first interview was free, and flashed her phone number across the screen. The results were dramatic. Within six weeks she signed up sixteen clients for various types of financial planning work.

Identify and Measure Market Impact
In Maureen's case it was very easy to measure the market impact of her television advertising. In other cases, however, results may be camouflaged or realized over an extended period of time. Nevertheless, knowing the impact a specific advertising program has on the targeted market is crucial to judging whether to change the approach, continue the same program, or abandon it completely.

To identify market impact and hence the amount of cashflow generated by the advertising campaign, especially over a long term, a monitoring system should be set up. It doesn't have to be complicated to be effective. In fact, the simpler the better. No prescribed format works universally. Each company, each advertising campaign, each marketing objective varies. As long as you come up with a system that incorporates two features it should work.

The monitoring system must be able to measure quantifiable results against original expectations. In other words, if you expect to see a sales increase of 10 percent over the next six months resulting from a direct mail campaign, you must be able to monitor where the new customers came from. In some companies this is easy. Just ask the customer what brought him or her to your company. Either the advertising brought them or it didn't. Other companies must take a broader approach, especially to monitor long-term results. If sales increase and you can't identify any other reason, then the advertising campaign gets the nod.

Second, to effectively monitor advertising results over a long term, some type of milestone measurement must be used. For example, if the objective is to increase market share by 6 percent over the next three years, an advertising campaign today will have little effect two and one-half years from now. But it could have an indirect effect by getting new customers now, which stimulates repeat business and other new customers later on.

A six-month measuring system that records new customers should reflect a big jump the first period, then a tapering off over the next four or five periods. If no increase in customers is realized the first six months, chances are good that the advertising failed to achieve its objective.

Control Advertising Expenses
Seven types of expenses, excluding payroll and benefits, account for 90 percent of most small business advertising budgets.

1. Printing for letterhead and envelopes for direct mail

2. Postage

3. Media charges (television, radio, newspapers, magazines, etc.)

4. Layouts, artwork, and copy

5. Color printing for brochures, etc.

6. Collating and assembling circulars, brochures, etc.

7. Recording and handling replies

A good rule of thumb is that any portion of this work handled by an advertising agency will cost at least 50 percent more, and in many cases 10 times more, than if you do the work yourself. The following represents comparisons of two advertising jobs I did for myself using my personal computer and an old, second hand offset press compared to similar jobs that I contracted with a small advertising agency to handle.

Case Number One

	In-House	Ad Agency
Direct mailing (500 mailings)		
Copy	0	$200
Letterhead and envelopes	$60	70
Print letterhead and envelopes	0	50
Address envelopes	0	120
Stuff envelopes	0	250
Collate and handle replies	0	250
Postage	125	125
Total cost	$185	$1,065

Case Number Two

	In-House	Ad Agency
Two color, 4 x 6, 3-page brochure (500 copies)		
Copy	0	$500
Layout	0	600
Artwork	0	—
Printing (I could not do this myself)	600	1,000
Heavy paper	100	—
Total cost	$700	$2,100

You can count on large agencies from New York or other large metropolitan areas to cost a great deal more—probably five to ten times that of a small agency—assuming you could even get a large firm to handle small jobs.

Between state-of-the-art advances in short-run printing equipment and simplified personal computer software there is little reason to pay exorbitant prices to advertising agencies for direct mailings or black-and-white brochures. Direct contact with media advertisers gets a bit trickier but, as described later in this chapter, can also be accomplished without an agency.

Another reason to go with do-it-yourself advertising is that few agencies are so knowledgeable about your business that they have better ideas than you do about what advertising will work and what won't. Assuming you can keep the cost down, if direct mail doesn't work, try a newspaper ad. If that falls flat perhaps a spread in a trade publication. If all else fails maybe your best bet is to rely on a strong public relations program (which we'll look at later in this chapter). Without the added profit tacked on by advertising agencies, you can experiment until something does work and still not spend a fortune.

Equipment and Software
A few pieces of office equipment, a couple of good software packages, and layout and artwork assistance from independent contractors and any small business can put together its own advertising agency. The following equipment should be the minimum configuration for complete independence:

1. A personal computer with at least a 20 megabyte hard drive and one million bytes of random access memory (RAM). I prefer the IBM System 2 or compatible but Apple computers are also good. You can get a PC/2 for under $2,000 new or $1,200 used. Macintosh computers are about 50 percent more.

2. A laser printer with speed and print quality similar to the Hewlett Packard Laserjet II series. A new one

at under $1,000 or a used one at about $700 would be adequate.

3. A copy machine with multiple copy loading and (preferably) collating capabilities. Be sure it produces high-quality copies for long runs. Because of maintenance problems, it's best to lease one of these.

4. A facsimile machine. Be sure it runs at high speed and is compatible with common brands. A fax comes in handy for relaying documents to media or advertising agencies for special jobs.

5. A small offset press. A used one works perfectly fine. There are plenty of them around for less than $1,000.

6. An appropriate drafting table and art supplies.

In addition to equipment, special computer software must be purchased. Three packages should be sufficient.

1. A multiprogram desktop publishing package. Ventura by Xerox works great with IBM machines (under $700). Macintoshes have their own software. It is more expensive but also more user friendly.

2. A strong word-processing package. WordStar, WordPerfect, and Word are all capable of doing nearly anything (about $500).

3. A compatible telecommunications module to upload (transfer) data to media and agencies as needed. Hayes still has the premier model although others are also acceptable ($150).

It's always preferable to purchase new software rather than get it second hand. The manufacturer offers technical advice; and a complete instruction manual comes with the package. However, even though it is strictly illegal under the patent laws, many people continue to copy these programs for their personal use or to give to friends. Obviously, there is no technical help, warranty, or user manual with copied software.

Quick Print Shops

For those who don't like computers or who don't want to bother with all this equipment, state-of-the-art quick print shops offer an alternative. No longer restricted to copy machines, the new quick-print shops have a complete configuration of the above equipment plus much more. They are usually located within easy driving distance in most metropolitan areas and many smaller towns. To save time I occasionally use a franchise shop called AlphaGraphics (the franchise headquarters is located in Phoenix). The one located near my office is extremely capable, fast, and turns out a very high-quality product.

Using quick-print shops is more expensive than doing it yourself, but far less than using an advertising agency. A few have multicolor press capabilities and more are adding it every month. Charges for multicolor printing approximate what small printing companies charge.

Mailing Lists

Mailing lists are another do-it-yourself aid. With a good word-processing package and a printer capable of handling mailing labels, there is no reason to pay an agency to prepare mailings. Hundreds of reputable mailing list companies exist throughout the country. These companies will produce a mailing list by virtually any category of company, industry, geographic area, or product designation. Most of the bigger houses can do it either in hard copy mailing labels ready to stick on envelopes or computer disks for you to make your own labels. The latter is about half the price of having the labels preprinted.

Check you local yellow pages for mailing list companies nearby or a library reference desk for names and addresses of national firms. Mailing lists are expensive, however. A single sort list complete with first and last names of appropriate contacts runs between $1,000 and $2,000 for a minimum of 1,000 companies. Preprinted labels are extra.

Media Contacts

To a large extent placing media advertisements remains under the jurisdiction of advertising agencies. Legal collusion between major newspapers, magazines, television channels, and radio stations on the one hand and advertising agencies on the other makes placing your own ads a difficult undertaking. But it can be done. All it takes is perseverance, patience, and an apprentice's knowledge of media language. Two clients taught me how it's done.

> Jeramy ran a business brokerage company and wanted to place a series of advertisements in his local big-city newspaper. I recommended that he hire a small agency, another client, to do the placement for him but the broker wanted to save his cash. On calling the newspaper, the broker learned that the blocked ad with logo and special trim required a plate. The newspaper recommended he get an ad agency to handle it. The broker persisted and eventually was told exactly what he needed. It wasn't a plate at all but merely a typeset copy that he asked a local quick print shop to make with its desktop publishing software. It took some pulling but the exercise saved the broker about $500.

Another example occurred when a fast-food client was told by the local television channel that he needed a professionally prepared video for the station to run. The client borrowed a camcorder from his neighbor and made the video himself at one-fifth the cost of having an agency do the job.

It may not be as easy as advertising through direct mail, but media placement can also be a do-it-yourself activity. When times are tough every dollar saved adds up. Advertising is one activity where expenses can be cut to the bone and still be effective.

Choosing the Right Advertising Agency for the Job

If you do want to use an advertising agency, however, there is a wide range to choose from. Some are very good; some are very bad. Size doesn't seem to matter. I've know a few excellent agencies with two or three employees. I've also seen some bad ones. The same holds true for the giants: some are excellent, some terrible.

Small businesses, however, run into difficulty when they try to contract with a major agency. These firms are just too big and have too many large corporate accounts to be bothered with a small job. Even if they are interested, most are very difficult to work with because small jobs are pushed down the line to junior people. It's like working with a giant law firm. You may get an initial appointment with a senior partner but juniors will always do the work.

That being the case, it makes a lot more sense to go with an agency that is small enough that you can work directly with the owner. Then if you have any complaints, you'll know who to talk to!

The best way to locate a qualified small agency is through personal contacts. Ask around. Check with local businesses for references. If all else fails, local printing companies that work with advertising agencies always have their preferences. Be careful going this route though. It's entirely possible that the printing company gets a kickback from the agency if it brings in a new client, and that increases prices.

Try Cooperative Advertising

Cooperative advertising has become a popular way for small businesses to cut expenses. Several variations of the theme exist. Many franchisers place advertisements and publish sales brochures for franchisees. A few trade associations support group advertising for members, especially at trade shows. Local chambers of commerce and other business groups sponsor group advertising.

The major advantages in going with one of these group sponsors is cost and time. The cost of group advertising to each participant is always less than going it alone. The time and effort to set up and manage an advertising campaign or a trade show booth can be significant. Letting a group sponsor handle the details saves an enormous amount of time and effort, especially for one-person businesses.

Like everything else, however, you get what you pay for. Advertising sponsored by a formal trade, civic, or industry organization or a franchiser seldom brings the market control results necessary to support protective marketing strategies. If you can possibly afford even a modest advertising program on your own, chances are high you'll get better results.

A cross between formal group advertising and doing it yourself is rapidly becoming popular in certain industries in specific parts of the country. Companies producing similar products or selling into similar markets (not competitors) combine their major advertising budgets and in this way get bigger and farther-reaching campaigns than any of them could afford to do individually. Small companies in the toy industry started this approach several years ago and now it has spread to other industries.

Small manufacturers of wooden pull toys, plastic and rubber dolls, and miniature metal cars all sold to major department stores. Since none of them could advertise effectively against the industry giants they decided to combine resources and send joint fliers, posters, and other circulars to major retailers. They also combined their booths at the annual New York toy show. The system still seems to be working. Their efforts are certainly not as effective as individual programs would be, but they report that they believe results are better than going through a trade program.

Implement a Cost-Effective Public Relations Program

The other side of the publicity coin is public relations. For many businesses a well-managed advertising campaign is all they need or want to support their marketing efforts. For others, however, without a meaningful public relations program, advertising falls flat. In still other cases, advertising is too expensive and companies rely exclusively on public relations to sell their name and product.

Public relations is nothing more or less than creating a favorable image in the public eye. For many service businesses, reputation in the marketplace can make or break the company. Health care providers, investment advisors, physical fitness providers, literary agents, tax return preparers, and many other small service businesses prosper or fail because of their public reputation rather than because of any unique service they offer. Although some service businesses try to get their message across through advertising, many more rely on favorable public relations in their industry or in the public arena to generate business.

If concrete results from an advertising campaign are difficult to measure, specific benefits from a public relations program are virtually impossible to identify. Most business owners look to public relations (PR) as creating sustaining benefits over long periods of time.

Implementing a Public Relations Program
There are two ways to implement a cost-effective, sustaining public relations program to augment protective marketing strategies:

☐ Hire a professional PR firm to design and manage the program.

☐ Do it yourself.

The yellow pages from any metropolitan area lists a number of local public relations firms. Businesses that need national coverage, however, tend to use those located in New York, Chicago, or Los Angeles. Markets for certain businesses center around specific regions of the country and the most effective public relations can be obtained from firms located in those cities. If your business relates to publishing, for example, New York is the place to get a PR firm. Los Angeles still commands the lead for anyone in entertainment or leisure-time related businesses. Houston or Dallas own the oil-related industries.

Chicago is best for heavy industry, agriculture, and food processing.

Nearly all large corporations maintain continuing contracts with equally large PR firms. Stay away from these. They employ qualified people, all right, but the fees they charge are definitely not cost-effective for smaller companies. If you decide to go with a professional PR firm, try to zero in on one of the hundreds of capable small ones; generally one- or two-person businesses. Even with a smaller PR firm, however, a continuing program can easily run $2,000 per month on a one-year contract. Project work generally starts at $10,000 and goes up from there.

Using a public relations professional does have some definite advantages, assuming you can find a reliable one who has the same work standards as you. Several unethical PR professionals dot the landscape and are sometimes difficult to ferret out. A careful interviewing process should resolve this issue, however.

Once a reputable professional is chosen, he or she can either work on a project basis or on a continuing contract. A PR professional will design the program, and make all arrangements for implementation, whether it be television or radio interviews, media promotions, or lecture engagements.

Frequently public relations projects overlap with advertising programs. So much the better. A small publisher might run an advertising campaign directed at selling specialty magazines to homemakers and simultaneously have a PR firm line up interviews with these same magazines.

The two biggest advantages in using a professional rather than doing PR work yourself are (1) they know specifically who to contact to arrange promotions in any media, and (2) they do all the selling and administrative legwork, which can be very time consuming. The big disadvantage is that professionals cost money and in tough times scarce cash may be used more efficiently elsewhere.

Do-It-Yourself Public Relations
Professional PR firms are not necessary to create a favorable public image, however. Most small business owners can do it

themselves if they are willing and able to spare the time away from productive activities. Although most people certainly don't have the time or the inclination to implement a broad, sustaining PR program, specific targeted activities that don't take much effort can definitely help to establish a favorable public image.

One example of such do-it-yourself publicity was undertaken by Fred Petersen who prepared and sold an investment newsletter to 11,000 executive subscribers.

> Fred wanted to open a new market with college students in the nation's business schools. He couldn't afford to hire a PR firm but realized that to tap this market he must spread his reputation as an honest, knowledgeable investment advisor to the college ranks.
>
> Fred accomplished his objective in three steps. First he arranged to give a series of three free lectures on personal investing in the evening school division of a local college. Second, he arranged with the local newspaper to cover the lectures. Third he used this publicity to convince seven of the largest business school magazines that were circulated to college students to publish his article about investment projections.
>
> Fred managed the entire PR program without spending a dollar, except for minor travel expenses and postage. Within a year he had created a new market and netted over 4,000 subscribers from the college ranks.

The starting point in developing a publicity campaign is to establish your reputation as an expert in your field. This means building credentials in the marketplace. This can be accomplished in a number of ways depending on a person's communication skills, the area of expertise, and market dispersion (local, regional, national, or international).

Some specialties offer optional certification or licensing (e.g., financial planning, public accounting, life and casualty insurance, auto mechanics). Getting certified automatically establishes a level of competence in the public eye. Other fields lend themselves to written publications (e.g., letters to the editor, articles in trade publications, articles in bank, insurance company, or tax newsletters). Still others accent participation in group events (e.g., trade shows, public forums, symposiums, panel discussions).

With credentials in hand, a PR program can begin. Some do-it-yourself PR steps cost a few dollars. Others can be done with no out-of-pocket expenditures. The following methods for getting publicity for yourself or your company cost at worst a few hundred dollars. Most are free. Some are particularly adaptable to small service businesses. Others lend themselves to retail establishments. Still others seem to work best for manufacturing businesses.

Ideas For Publicity Campaigns

1. Invite a local newspaper to write an article on some unique aspect of the company.

2. Invite television reporters to cover a special event sponsored by the company (e.g., a fund-raising drive, a banquet honoring an employee, a snappy new product).

3. Start a charity book collection drive at local schools.

4. Sponsor a young people's athletic team.

5. Sponsor a civic band or float in a local parade.

6. Donate materials, space, or services to community theater groups.

7. Provide facilities for boy/girl scout, Rotary, Kiwanis, Toastmaster, or other public or civic groups.

8. Sponsor a paper, glass, aluminum, or plastic recycling drive.

9. Get behind a social cause (e.g., homes for the homeless, food and clothing drives for the poor, clothing and activity donations for state mental hospitals).

10. Donate used computers, office equipment, and so on to local schools, hospitals, welfare agencies.

Personal Public Imaging
The main idea in a public relations program is to create a favorable public image. The reverse can also happen—an unfavorable image. Companies selling products in markets deemed environmentally or socially harmful have an especially difficult time maintaining a favorable image. One of the best ways to overcome this stigma is to take an active, positive public role in community or political affairs. Demonstrating public responsibility can frequently overcome at least some of the tarnish. Following are a few ideas that you might experiment with to improve the public image of yourself and your company with minimal, if any, cash expenditure.

Ideas For Public Imaging

1. Run for local public office.

2. Speak to local school or community groups about drug abuse, alcoholism, teen pregnancy, and so on.

3. Start a new Rotary, Kiwanis, or other social help chapter.

4. Become active in your local PTA group (if you have school-age children).

5. Write social or political commentary articles for the local newspaper.

6. Become an active leader in your church.

7. Conduct a lecture series on community topics.

8. Teach an adult evening class.

9. Lead a fund-raising drive for the United Way, Heart Association, or other charitable organization.

10. Participate in radio and television talk shows.

The whole idea behind public imaging is to project a sense of caring and participation about and in community events. Obviously, if your markets are national rather than local this type of imaging won't buy much. On the other hand, more than one entrepreneur has parlayed local community involvement into national recognition as a political or social leader. And this does improve market recognition on a scale beyond the immediate locale.

Summary

Well-conceived and conscientiously managed advertising and public relations programs are integral tools of a protective marketing strategy. Businesses of all sizes and in virtually any industry need to seriously implement either an advertising campaign or a public relations program, or both, to ensure market control. Unfortunately, smaller companies tend to shy away from both advertising and public relations. They assume the expense is too great to fit tough-times budgets, or they erroneously cut existing advertising and PR budgets to conserve cash.

Since advertising is an important tool to bring new customers to the market, to capture customers from competitors, or to provide market intelligence, a way must be found to make it cost effective and affordable to even the smallest company. To implement a cost-effective advertising campaign four objectives must be met: (1) the type of advertising must be consistent with protective marketing objectives; (2) its focus must be on achieving the greatest market impact in the shortest time frame; (3) actual results from the advertising campaign must be monitored against expected results; and (4) expenses incurred for the campaign must be kept to a minimum.

A basic principle in cost-effective advertising is to select only those media and types of advertising that are really needed. Too much advertising or the wrong type is wasted money and effort. A small advertising agency can get the job done with a minimum involvement from the business owner, but many times using an agency is just too expensive. Do-it-yourself advertising can be done with the proper configuration of office equipment, principally through the use of word-processing and desktop publishing personal computer software.

State-of-the-art quick-print shops are useful for taking up the slack. Mailing lists for practically any industry, product line, or region are easily accessible. Direct media contacts are also possible, although occasionally it takes some fancy footwork. You can also use cooperative advertising through industry trade groups, franchisers, or local chambers of commerce to cut advertising expenses without getting involved yourself. Cooperative efforts between compatible local businesses also works.

The purpose of a public relations program is to develop a favorable public image of your company or yourself or both. Professional PR firms are effective but they are also expensive. When putting together a PR program for your company, focus on supporting community activities. It may be necessary to develop a socially conscious public image to overcome adverse publicity if your product offering conflicts with environmentally or socially sensitive areas.

Regardless of the form of advertising campaigns or public relations programs, companies of any size benefit from the active use of these marketing tools. With a little effort and creativity nearly anyone can design and manage his or her own public and customer awareness slates.

With protective marketing strategies in place and advertising and public relations programs as tools, the next step is to structure cost-effective selling policies. The next chapter presents some ideas and tips for doing just that.

Chapter 7

Survival Selling
Low-Cost Sales Tactics That Work

Strategies aimed at recession-proofing market control are essential. Advertising and public relations campaigns are important supporting tools for spreading the word about your company's products, services, and reputation. But neither strategies nor tools will increase cash-flow by themselves. Ultimately, they must be used to bring in profitable sales. This chapter examines a series of selling tactics that translate protective marketing strategies into higher sales and cost reductions into cash savings. These tactics can be conveniently grouped under four headings.

- ☐ Tactics to increase sales volume
- ☐ Tactics to speed up cash collections
- ☐ Tactics to reduce selling expenses
- ☐ Tactics to induce greater selling efforts

Tactics to Increase Sales Volume
Almost any business can increase its sales by lowing prices sufficiently below competition to attract price-conscious buyers. As a short-term tactic, price cutting is an effective tool to achieve a specific market purpose. As long as volume increases in propor-

tion to the corresponding drop in unit margin, you benefit. At least until competition retaliates.

In a buyer's market, prices remain depressed and margins low. A price decrease invariably brings quick retaliatory action by competitors. As prices continue to drop, margins whither away and soon bankruptcies proliferate the industry.

On the other hand, in a seller's market competitors quickly learn that dropping prices really doesn't get them much increased volume. The only result is lower profits. In both buyer's and seller's markets, long-term price decreases lead to trouble. Certainly, in tough times, when the objective is to recession-proof a company, dropping prices only aggravates the problem by bringing in less cash than previously. This translates into less cash; the reverse of what is needed.

Many ways exist to increase sales volume without wholesale price cutting. Whether your business is product or service oriented, developing sales tactics to increase volume through one of these other methods always results in a healthier company. The fundamental principle behind tactics to increase sales volume is that a greater number of customers broadens a customer base over the long haul, increases market share, and thus improves market control.

Promotional efforts that encourage higher quantity buying by the same customer base achieve short-term results, but unless buying habits can be altered, eventually customers slip back to their old ways. This doesn't imply that short-term, volume-buying tactics are wrong. In fact as a method for raising quick cash they work very well. A well rounded recession-proof sales program however, should incorporate long-term market control tactics as well as short-term cash gains.

Although sales promotion efforts vary significantly by size of company, geographic coverage, and type of product or service, the following tactics can be implemented by a great number of businesses. It's important to recognize that these tactics are only illustrative of what can be done. They should, however, stimulate ideas applicable to your business. These tactics to increase profitable sales consist of:

☐ Volume pricing

☐ Incentive returns

☐ Rapid delivery

☐ Customer training

☐ Barter

Later in this chapter we'll explore a program to implement and manage sales promotions with minimum cash expenditures.

Volume Pricing
We are all familiar with how volume pricing works. If you normally buy one pair of shoes for $100 and a sales promotion offers a second pair for $5, each pair of shoes actually costs $52.50. Or if customers usually buy one can of oil for $2 and a special promotion offers a case of 12 for $18 the cost per can drops to $1.50. Volume pricing promotions in retail businesses are commonplace and have been commonplace for years.

Most retail establishments that offer such discounts do so for a short time only. The promotions are usually paid for by the manufacturer or distributor so the retailer doesn't suffer any loss of margin. Permanent volume pricing in retailing is not as common, however. In fact, during tough times and without support from distributors or manufacturers, most retailers retract volume pricing promotions.

This might be the wrong approach. If a retailer has market control in a specific product or line of products, volume pricing may be just the ticket to encourage additional sales. It can also be an effective retailing ploy over the very short-term even if you don't have market control, as a small Midwest retailer found out.

A small retailer of automobile aftermarket products tried volume pricing when sales were lagging and realized substantial results. The retailer arranged to receive a triple shipment of four types of windshield ice scrapers at a 35 percent discount. Wal-Mart, Kmart and several other large discounters in the area carried these lines but priced them the same as during the previous winter. With the 35 percent purchase discount in hand, the small retailer knocked 50 percent off the Wal-Mart scraper price and ran a promotion piece in the local newspaper. Two weeks later he sold out—one day before Wal-Mart and the others dropped their prices.

Service businesses tend to stay away from volume pricing, mainly because many have not analyzed how to offer volume services. Some service businesses are eminently adaptable to volume pricing, however.

A perfect example of this occurred with the auto repair shop owned by Brad Snofel. Chapter 5 described how Brad turned smart customers into continuing repeat business.

> A year after he explained his secret to his competitor across the street, Brad's business was growing so fast he decided to expand his facility. He located an appropriate building one block away and converted it into a second shop.
>
> Brad staffed the new shop with three mechanics and shuffled overload business down the block. He had misjudged his volume, however. The first shop kept busy but the new shop only had enough business to keep one mechanic busy full time and the other two part time.
>
> Rather than lay off a qualified mechanic, Brad came up with a volume pricing scheme. For regular maintenance work—oil changes, lube jobs, state inspections, minor tune-ups, and so on—Brad offered to do the same work on a customer's second car for half price. As word spread the shop filled up in no time. Brad continues his volume discount policy to this day and is just about ready to open a third shop.

This same volume pricing philosophy can be extended to many other service businesses. A tax return preparer can offer discounts for multiple returns from the same family. The same idea works for dentists. Dry cleaners can use two-for-one sales on women's or men's suits. Lawn-cutting services can offer discount pricing for handling all the lawns in a given neighborhood. Even authors take discounted royalties for multiple book contracts.

Some volume pricing promotions turn into permanent discounting, as in the case of Brad Snofel. Others are effective for short periods, as in the case of the ice-scraper retailer. If volume pricing fits your business it can be an effective tool to increase sales, and thus cash, when other methods fail. At least it's worth considering.

Incentive Returns

Incentive return promotions work well in retail and manufacturing businesses but I have never seen it applied to a service business. That doesn't mean it won't work there, however, given the right circumstances. Incentive return policies are based on the premise that if a customer doesn't like the product it can be returned with no questions asked. For years Sears has applied this policy to sales of its Craftsman line of hand and power tools, as well as other selected products. Unquestionably, this policy has kept the Craftsman line at or near the top of small tool markets.

An incentive return policy promotion can also be used as a sales gimmick over a short term. For example, assume you own a manufacturing company assembling electronic widgets sold to discount department stores. You come up with a new product, a programmable mileage device attachable to a car's dashboard that records the exact amount of toll charges as the car approaches each exit on a tollroad. The advantage of course, is that it is difficult to read the small print on the toll tickets used by the tollroads. The apparatus reads the toll based on miles traveled between tollgates.

Further assume that sales of this hot device have been slow. Recessionary pressures force chain stores to restrict their buying of new products. A major question is how to get these stores to buy the toll recorder without cutting prices. One way is a promotion to guarantee full refunds if a chain store can't sell the product and if it returns the products within 30 days. If the product really does meet a market need, there shouldn't be too many returns. However, the fact that stores have the option of a money-back guarantee induces them to give the product a chance.

Of course, money-back guarantee promotions can also backfire. If the promotion is very successful in stimulating new sales and at the same time a large number of customers return them, it can cost much more than other types of promotions. This shouldn't happen with existing products because presumably they are already accepted in the market. But it might very well occur with a new product introduction. Several retail stores have learned the hard way not to use this promotion with juvenile furniture, dolls, and toys. Too many of the products are poorly constructed and unless backed by the same return policy from the manufacturer, stores can get stuck with a pile of useless, broken merchandise.

Same-Day Delivery
Same-day delivery or same-day service are excellent promotional schemes for increasing sales at very little additional expense. As our economy becomes increasingly more attuned to the buy-it-now, have-it-now attitude, we become more and more frustrated with waiting days, many times weeks, for our product to arrive or service to be done. These conditions make same-day deliveries an extraordinarily effective sales tactic.

Increasingly time is money, yet few suppliers pay any attention to rapid service. Everyone wants his bills paid on time but few merchants reciprocate. A postal system that requires four days to fly a letter from New York to Los Angeles and three days to transport a letter 90 miles from New York to Philadelphia seems to reflect the general lack of concern for product delivery service in our economy.

Promotions promising same-day delivery or service within a specific area almost always bring in new customers for retailers, manufacturers, and service companies alike. For some businesses, however, same-day delivery is impossible.

In my consulting business, for example, it is physically impossible to deliver a report to a client the same day I do they work, and of course clients realize this. But I have learned to follow a similar principle. When I promise a client a report by nine o'clock on Wednesday, I make sure it is there at that time.

Doing what you say you are going to do, when you promise you will do it, at least in many service businesses, increases sales as effectively as rapid delivery in product businesses. It is simply good public relations. Turning it around, when a plumber, electrician, or furnace repair person tells me they will service my call tomorrow and they actually do it, I will certainly return to the same company for service next time around—assuming the work was properly done.

Customer Training

Some businesses sell technical products that require a certain amount of expertise on the part of customers to use the products. A case in point would be personal computer software. Many software retailers offer customer training classes in how to use the programs. Also, most of them charge fairly high prices for this training. A short-term sales promotion offering free customer training classes is a great way to sell more software, as Mary Todd discovered.

> Mary Todd ran a software store in a Philadelphia suburb. Software was her only product. She didn't handle computers, printers, or any other hardware, nor did she offer repair service. Just software. Competition was fierce. New stores were opening every week that offered software sales along with hardware and repair services. Even the large department stores were in on the act. Mary's business was going downhill fast. She needed ideas for a creative sales promotion scheme.
>
> I suggested she circulate a flier to her customers from the past month and also post a large sign in her store announcing free training classes every Saturday morning for the next two months in Lotus 1-2-3, WordPerfect, and Ventura desktop publishing programs. The only stipulation for attendance was that the customer had to bring along a guest.
>
> The promotion was a rousing success. Not only did her customer list expand from the promotion effort, she also sold several software packages to the guests at the training classes. As a byproduct, the local division of a large corporation heard about the classes and contracted with Mary to conduct training classes at the division offices every Saturday morning for six months—this time for a substantial fee, of course.

Customer training promotions don't have to be free. As long as the fee charged is less than that of the competition, customer training is almost a surefire way to increase sales in many types of businesses. The best part about a customer training promotion is that, assuming you can do the training yourself (or you have an employee capable of doing it) it doesn't cost anything to implement, except perhaps some inexpensive advertising.

Cost-Effective Sales Promotions

Sales promotions are effective ways of increasing sales and if structured probably can cost very little to implement. Some expense is usually involved, however. It's hard to implement a sales promotion without advertising it. It's impossible to gain maximum benefits from a promotion without managing it. And in businesses with few if any employees, the time available to do justice to a sales promotion is practically nonexistent.

Before starting to spend money advertising a sales promotion, it's a good idea to think through the mechanics of how it will work and to establish what results can be expected from it. I find the following five step program-questionnaire extremely useful when working this problem through with clients.

Program-Questionnaire For Planning Sales Promotion

1. What do you expect to gain from this promotion?

    a. Increased sales from existing customers?

       How much?

       For how long?

    b. Increased customer base?

       How many new customers?

       Repeat customers?

       How much sales will they bring in?

    c. To introduce a new product/service?

       How much sales?

       What follow-up to the promotion?

    d. To open a new market?

       Where? What? How big?

       How long will it take?

2. What sales promotions are involved?

    a. Volume pricing?

    b. Incentive returns?

    c. Customized or same-day delivery?

    d. Customer training?

    e. Other? What type?

3. How will you notify the market of the sales promotion?

    a. Circulars? Mailing? Hand-delivered notices? Picked-up notices? How many?

    b. Newspaper advertising? What newspaper?

    c. Direct mail notification? How many?

    d. Television? Radio? Cassette tape? Video?

4. What is the cost?

    a. Advertising?

    b. Lost production time?

    c. Damaged merchandise?

    d. Rented space?

    e. Special equipment?

    f. Contract labor?

5. Who will manage the promotion?

    a. You?

    b. Sales manager?

     c. Other employee?

     d. Advertising agency? What cost?

     e. Other outsider? What cost?

Managing the Promotion

Question 5 brings up an important point. Many smaller businesses start a sales promotion without giving any thought to who will manage it. As with every activity in business, someone must be in charge. Someone must have the responsibility for putting all the pieces together and making sure the promotion gets implemented as planned. And someone must be accountable for the problems and miscalculations along the way that always occur.

In smaller companies, sales promotions nearly always work best if the business owner is in charge. You should be on the premises to greet customers if that's part of the promotion. You should coordinate and follow-up to make sure deliveries are made on time if that's part of the program. You should personally handle any barter arrangement or questions from customers. In larger companies a competent sales manager can manage a promotion, but in smaller companies its up to the owner.

Shared Promotions

As with the techniques for sharing market research and after-sales service activities examined in chapter 5, sharing sales promotions can substantially reduce out-of-pocket expenses. Retail and service businesses located in shopping malls often participate in promotional programs instituted by mall management. Neighborhood groups of businesses of varying types and sizes frequently combine resources to sponsor one-day or one-week sales promotions for everyone. Some trade associations reserve part of their operating budget to assist members to finance regional or national promotions.

In some industries competitors band together to promote pricing discounts or special services for specific markets and a definite time period. Restaurants are a prime example. Discount coupon books offering two meals for the price of one, one-half off on Tuesdays, special menus for children, or ethnic nights, are normally paid for jointly by participating restaurants in a given area. Smaller hotels use the same approach. When large convention groups come to town a group of hotels pays for promotional literature offering special services or discounts for conventioneers.

With little customer or product differentiation, smaller businesses are often better off sharing sales promotions with competitors than implementing individual promotions. More traffic can be attracted and the cost is always less.

Barter

As a means of conducting trade, barter has been around since cave dwellers existed. Although not used extensively in this country, bartering indigenous goods for imported goods is common practice in the Caribbean, the Far East and other developing areas. Barter is simply the exchange of one product or service for another without any cash changing hands. But how can barter be used as a tactic to increase cash-flow from sales? Through two mediums: public relations and the sale of exchanged property or goods.

A good example of how the public relations gimmick works comes from a personal experience while living on the island of St. Croix in the U.S. Virgin Islands.

> I had been in the merger and acquisition consulting business for several years before moving to St. Croix for health reasons. Shortly after arriving, I started a business brokerage company. Although sellers were plentiful, there weren't many buyers on the island. The reason was simple: there just wasn't much money in the economy and bank loans were scare and hard to get.
>
> I had plenty of free time in the beginning so I decided to start a computer school, teaching applications in spreadsheet, word processing, and accounting software. At that time computers were just coming to the island so my classes were very popular. But once again, money was scarce and most of my

students—secretaries, law clerks, retail store owners, librarians—didn't have extra cash. So I hit upon barter.

In exchange for computer lessons I received office furniture, typing and copying services, legal advice, printing, computer repair services, and several other items of value. More important, as an indirect benefit, I picked up four listings of businesses for sale, three potential business buyers, and several leads to money sources on the mainland.

The public relations value alone was worth the time and effort spent conducting classes. It was the type of publicity that could take a market newcomer many months to develop. And it didn't take any cash. In addition, of course, the exchanged goods and services conserved cash that would otherwise have been spent on these necessities.

The other side of the barter coin relates to picking up additional sales not otherwise available, and at potentially higher margins. Assume I own an office furniture distributorship and you own a company that distributes cut meat to restaurants. We agreed to exchange a desk, chair, and lamp worth $2,500 for various cuts of beef and pork.

I then make a deal with two restaurants in my neighborhood to take delivery of the meat from your warehouse and pay me $3,000, which is 10 percent below the price of similar cuts charged by the local meat packer. The two restaurants are happy with a 10 percent discount. You are happy with new office furniture. I'm happy because I have made an extra $500 profits above the margin on my furniture. A win-win-win situation for everyone.

This is a classic example of how to make money through barter deals. It sounds complex, but it really isn't. It does, however, demand an extra effort to locate appropriate buyers for the bartered goods. If that can be done without spending any cash, then barter is a surefire sales tactic to improve cash-flow.

Although barter won't always work for every company, many times it can be used effectively to stimulate sales of other products. Any repair business is ideally suited to barter arrangements. So are personal service businesses. At times it's hard to distinguish between public relations, advertising, and sales promotion, but whatever you want to call it, barter works.

Fortunately barter is still too nebulous, and probably confusing, for many larger competitors to use. Smaller companies seem to have far more success. In the global community, however, barter is a way of life. It will only be a short time before barter becomes a popular form of trade in this country as well. Some clear-cut tax advantages also exist in barter arrangements.

Probably the most difficult part of using barter as a promotion tactic is structuring an advertising program to let potential customers know of the type of barter arrangements you will take. Unfortunately, there isn't any easy way to do this. Soliciting barter sales takes creativity and a certain sophistication on the part of customers. Customers who have lived overseas or spent any time doing business in Third World countries will of course know how it works. The typical American consumer, however, will probably be leery of any barter overtures.

One way that seems effective is to run ads in local newspapers explaining what barter is all about and what your promotion involves. Also, several barter brokerages are being formed around the country. Keep your eyes and ears open. Perhaps your trade association knows of one.

Those are a few ideas for effective tactics to increase sales volume while minimizing cash outlays. They don't all work for all businesses. Some require modest cash outlays, others none. Every business owner has his or her own creative ideas for stimulating sales.

The whole idea behind recession-proof sales promotions is to choose those tactics that yield the greatest volume at the least cost for your specific business. What works for others, even in the same industry, may not work for you. But you will never know if you don't try. As long as expenses are kept at a minimum, experimenting with sales promotions is often the best and only way to find out what works.

In addition to sales promotions, three other recession-proofing selling topics need to be examined: collecting receivables, trimming selling costs, and motivating sales personnel.

Tactics That Work for Collecting Receivables

Every business that sells on credit eventually accumulates accounts that do not pay on time, or at all; and a sale is never completed until cash comes in the door. When times are tough, large as well as small customers in every industry try to delay paying their bills. Their tactics vary but the result is the same: less cashflow for a seller.

It doesn't seem to make any difference how much cash a large customer has on hand or how badly small sellers need to conserve their cash. During tough times every buyer stretches payables and every seller suffers the consequences. Chapter 12 hits upon some of the more creative ways to delay paying bills, but here we're concerned with the other side—collecting.

Small sellers always seem to be behind the eight ball. They need cash much more desperately than large customers yet they are afraid to push too much for fear of losing the customer. Subcontractors in the government contracting business know their prime contractor customers have collected from the government but are reticent to claim their share out of fear that the next contract will be awarded to a competitor. Sales representatives who are due commissions from large manufacturers sit back waiting to be paid for fear the supplier will alter its sales policies. Even authors, starved for cash, refuse to push a cash-rich Simon & Schuster or a McGraw-Hill for contractually due advances and royalties for fear of not getting another contract.

When times are tough, however, small business owners can't afford to play the nice guy. They can't afford to worry about the next order. They need their money now, and if they don't take stringent actions to collect amounts due they won't be in business very long. It takes courage to ask a customer for your money, but recession-proofing calls for it.

We have all struggled for years searching for effective collection procedures. For a while, collection agencies seemed to help. Then credit became too lax and the fear of a blemished credit record died. Dun & Bradstreet and other collection agencies are still used, but for a small business their effectiveness is certainly questionable. I have never collected any accounts this way in all the companies I have owned.

About the only leverage a small business has relates to repeat customers. You can always refuse to ship additional product or perform additional services until the past due account is paid. You run the risk of losing the customer, but that's less dangerous than not getting paid.

Other methods can hasten payment and completely avoid collection problems and more and more companies are using these methods. Following are a few of the creative methods smaller businesses are currently employing:

1. Require a 25 or 30 percent down payment with the order.

2. Sell only on cash or credit card terms.

3. Demand payment in full before releasing the order (COD terms).

4. Offer small price discounts for cash in advance.

5. Give a small discount for COD customer pickups.

6. Blame your inability to offer credit on your bank.

7. If the work extends over a period of time, demand progress payments (as in the building trades).

8. Get a co-signer to guarantee a customer's payment.

9. Factor your receivables and let the bank worry about collecting (but this is very expensive).

10. For large sales, get a personal guarantee from the buyer or outside collateral as security.

Regardless of the method, it's crucial for every seller to do whatever is necessary to get accounts paid when due. In addition to collecting receivables, recession-proofing requires that stringent controls be implemented over selling expenses.

Make Selling Expenses Pay

Sales people hate to have the boss watch their expenses. The age-old arguments from sales people never change: "I have to entertain my customers to close the order." "My customers insist I call on them personally." "How would it look if I took my customer to lunch in a three-year old car?" "All the coach seats were taken. I had to fly first class to keep my appointment." " The few expenses I incur are a small price to pay for all the orders I bring in." And on and on and on.

These statements may all be true. Nevertheless, when times are tough, cash expenditures for selling expenses must face the same scrutiny as production and administrative expenses. To complete the recession-proofing cost reduction program, selling activities must bear part of the load.

Other than advertising and public relations expenses covered in the previous chapter, the typical major categories of expenses relating the sales activities are

- □ Salespersons compensation and benefits
- □ Travel
- □ Customer entertainment and promotion
- □ Sales literature
- □ Telephone, fax, and telecommunications
- □ Company automobiles

Let's take a look at methods to reduce each of these expenses.

Sales Compensation and Benefits

Typically, salaries, bonuses, incentive payments, and related benefits represent the largest chunk of selling expenses. Later in this chapter we'll look at a creative way to control bonuses and incentive payments.

Many companies find that product mix, customer mix, sales promotions, and advertising campaigns—all those facets of market control—can be administered more effectively with salaried sales personnel. Job security, incentive programs, and pride of accomplishment by the salesperson, and your ultimate control over employees' actions all support the argument for maintaining a salaried sales force. In tough times, however, compromises must be made.

One compromise is to switch from salaried sales people to commissioned sales representatives. Commissioned sales reps only get paid if they bring in the sales and this eliminates paying for unproductive time. Also, properly structured, a sales representative agreement frequently ties the payment of commissions to collections from customers. Even though a rep books an order, commission isn't paid until the customer pays for the product or service. You save two ways: lower selling expenses, and collections help from the sales person.

Travel Expenses

Sales travel expenses are easy to control. In the first place, using commissioned sales people eliminates the entire expense, along with all other selling expenses. Commissioned representatives pay their own way. For salaried salespersons, however, or if you make out-of-town sales calls, travel expenses must be watched.

All plane reservations and ticketing should be done by a travel agent with strict instructions to book the cheapest discount fare—even if it means changing planes. Sales calls should be planned in advance to take advantage of 7-day and 14-day discount fares. Obviously such luxuries as first-class or business-class fares should be avoided completely. Traveling like a peasant may be uncomfortable, but you get to your destination just as fast and just as safe as the person sitting in the front seat drinking free cocktails.

Many companies earn a second benefit by booking through a travel agent. They arrange to carry an open account with the agency, thus allowing at least 30-days to pay the bill. Allowing a travel agent to charge on a company American Express credit card accomplishes the same purpose.

Stringent rules about renting cars should also be enforced. I've never seen an order lost because the sales person showed up in a compact rental car. Full-size rentals are more expensive and unnecessary, so insist that everyone uses the smallest car available. And don't take any insurance offered by the rental company. Either American Express, personal automobile policies, or fleet coverage takes care of rental cars also.

Stay out of first-class hotels. Once again, sales are seldom made simply because the salesperson stayed at a Hilton, Marriott, Sheraton, or Hyatt. Have the travel agent book rooms at Days Inns or other budget hotels. The savings is always significant.

It's too easy for sales people to spend more than necessary when traveling. Keep a tight rein on expense reports. Demand documentation. Insist sales people follow company travel policies. And make round trips whenever possible. Airline competition has made one-day trips a reality in most parts of the country. There is no need to incur unnecessary hotel and food expenses.

Customer Entertainment and Promotion

We all love to play the VIP with customers. It boosts our ego to pick up lunch or dinner tabs, supply liquor for sales parties, order expensive wine for dinner, and on and on. Just remember that current tax laws dictate that only 80 percent of entertainment expenses are deductible. So right off the bat you lose 20 percent.

Clearly, some entertaining is expected by customers. For some purchasing agents, the only time they get a chance to eat out is when a seller treats. But once again the temptation to overspend is hard to control. One of the best methods, although hated by salespersons, is to establish a maximum per diem allowance for entertaining—say $25 per day. If they want to play the VIP let them spend their own money. Tough times demand tough actions.

Another way is to pay for fully documented meals but no liquor or wine. If a salesperson wants to supply drinks he does it out of his or her own pocket. These measures might seem extreme. On the other hand, with tightened tax laws, dropping profits, and tough times all around, most smaller companies, and many large ones, have enacted policies to severely restrict customer entertaining. And many customers, in the same boat themselves, fully understand and accept the concept that if they really want to play, they must share in the expense.

Sales Literature

Chapter 6 recommended tactics to reduce the cost of designing and printing advertising copy. These same procedures apply to sales literature. With word-processing and desktop publishing software, and perhaps a small offset press, nearly all sales literature can be prepared in-house at one-tenth the cost of having it done on the outside. Price lists, promotion circulars, even product brochures can be designed and printed internally. Maybe it requires cutting back from a four-color brochure to a two-color one, but that shouldn't affect booking the sale.

Control of the supply of sales literature is also important. Sales persons love to carry quantities of everything when calling on customers. They leave price lists and product brochures even if the customer doesn't want them or already has some from the last call. The more paper carried around, the more dog-eared it gets, and consequently the more of it gets thrown out.

Restrict the quantities of each type of literature each sales person can have. Make them sign out for fresh batches. Keep an inventory of what you have. A simple columnar pad will do. Keep changes in format to a minimum. Change the format or content of new brochures only when the old one is out-of-date. Mark up old price sheets with new prices rather than printing new ones each time. Just as with every other operating expense, sales literature can be controlled with a little effort.

Telephone, Fax, Telecommunications

Telephone and communication expenses are easy to control. Insist that everyone account for each call made or each message by fax. Since these expenses are budgeted in your cost reduction program, you'll have something to match the actual usage against. If one month exceeds budget, take action.

Salespersons love to talk on the phone almost as much as they enjoy entertaining. Take away their phone and their fax, and sales people are lost. There is no reason why they can't live within their budget however. After all, they had a hand in preparing it in the first place.

Company Cars
In this day and age most salespersons are given a company car as part of their compensation package. A company car is a terrific employee benefit, but it always costs more than one realizes. And for obvious reasons, employees are not as careful caring for a car if the company owns it.

Following are a few ideas for reducing the expense of company cars for salespersons. Many will meet with resistance but they all reduce expenses. Tough times, tough actions.

1. Charge the employee a monthly fee for personal use of the car.

2. Insist employees pay part of the fleet insurance premium.

3. Have employees insure the car under a personal policy with partial reimbursement from the company.

4. Charge all gasoline and repairs on company credit cards and then insist on a monthly accounting of trips.

5. Have employees pay for their own gas and repairs with partial reimbursement by the company.

6. Lease the fleet with a open-end lease.

7. Lease the cars for four or five years rather than three.

8. Use only compact cars in the fleet.

9. Charge employees for repairs that result from road accidents.

Motivate with Sales Incentives

The final step in structuring cost-effective sales tactics is to implement an incentive plan for salaried sales personnel. An incentive plan is especially necessary when many of the benefits enjoyed by salespersons have been reduced. The last thing you want to do is demoralize your sale force. I can't think of any more certain way for a company to fail.

Sales incentive plans come in all sizes and shapes. Some are expensive to administer, some simple. Some are effective, others are a waste of time and money. Some might be effective if the sales personnel could understand how they worked, but their complexity makes them inoperable.

Similar to employee incentive plans described in chapters 3 and 4, a meaningful sales incentive plan should consist of three carefully conceived elements:

1. Goals that can be controlled by the salesperson (i.e., specific sales levels per month and specific expense budgets).

2. A simple method to measure the results accurately and timely against the goals.

3. An award that is important to the individual.

Goals should be established jointly between a salesperson and the owner. Goals can be sales levels, expense levels, product margins, sales promotion results, or any other quantifiable objective that can be controlled by the salesperson without interference from you or other personnel. These goals should be incorporated into a sales and profit forecast by month, and related to the applicable period. The shorter time frame to reach goals the better. That's why monthly forecasts (or budgets) seem to work fairly well.

The forecast and budgets become the standard against which to measure performance. Since monthly goals have been jointly established with sales personnel, the salesperson must believe that they can be attained. If they don't believe this, the plan won't work. Each month the results of performance against plan should be relayed to each salesperson so they know exactly where they stand. If they miss one month, maybe they can make up for it the next.

Finally, the rewards granted upon achieving these goals must be important to the recipient. A gold watch might sound terrific but if the employee already has four watches it won't mean much. The range of options for rewards are limitless.

As a critical step in setting up the incentive plan, sit down with each employee and decide together what the employee wants and whether the company can afford it. There is nothing wrong with different rewards for different employees. Some may want cash, others time off from work, still others a dinner out with a mate. As long as you can afford the cash outlay, allowing each employee to set his or her own incentive award increases the effectiveness of an incentive plan immeasurably.

By translating protective marketing strategies and cost-effective advertising and public relations programs into sales-generating policies, you will have completed the second leg of a total recession-proof program. Cost reductions and more higher-margin sales will go a long way toward improving your cash-flow. Simultaneously with implementing these policies it doesn't hurt to clean up your facility and sell off all that old equipment and obsolete inventory. The next chapter suggests methods to maximize cash in this area as the third recession-proofing step.

Chapter 8

Trim Back Assets

Converting Equipment and Space to Cash

Surviving tough times not only means cutting costs and hitting the market hard, it also means trimming back assets. Trimming back assets can be accomplished by selling and then leasing back those hard assets that are necessary to function as a business, or it can be done by selling any asset that is not crucial to business survival.

Nearly every business has some assets it uses to operate. Perhaps only a desk, lamp, and telephone—although it's difficult to raise cash with these few assets. Nearly all manufacturing companies own machinery, vehicles, office equipment, furniture and fixtures, and inventory. Retail businesses can hardly operate without store fixtures, office equipment and furniture, and inventory. Service business may be restricted to office equipment and furniture and perhaps automobiles.

It seems that the longer a company is in business, the more hard assets are left to accumulate dust. Now is the time to do something productive with them. Now is the time to convert them into cash.

Now is also the time to take a second look at sale/leaseback possibilities. Although it doesn't get much press any more, the leasing industry is alive and well. Several national and international leasing companies have built their businesses through sale/leaseback deals.

A third way to convert assets to cash has become very popular with service businesses—leasing out unused storage, office, or production space. Other companies also trying to cut costs are always on the lookout for office or storage space they can rent at less than they are paying now.

This chapter explores these and several other ideas for trimming back assets to raise cash. Since selling off unneeded assets usually returns the greatest amount of cash, that's probably a good place to start. Five categories of assets each require different approaches:

☐ Production machinery and equipment

☐ Office equipment, furniture, and fixtures

☐ Vehicles

☐ Inventory

☐ Real property

Sell Production Machinery and Equipment
Nearly every manufacturing company has machinery and equipment it doesn't use. Machinery purchased for a special order that is now completed. Excess equipment left over after pruning product lines. Broken pieces that have never been repaired. Forklifts gathering dust after changing warehousing procedures. Machines that have been replaced with newer, state-of-the-art pieces.

It would be surprising if you didn't have some old or broken machines or equipment sitting in storage, in the corner, outside your plant, or at customers' facilities that are no longer needed. Now is the time to gather these pieces and sell them off.

The starting point is obviously a physical inventory of machinery and equipment you own. When making the count, segregate those pieces leased for a special job or borrowed from customers or neighbors. Although these won't bring cash, returning leased equipment will certainly reduce expenditures by stopping lease payments. And returning borrowed pieces will free floor space that may be rented out to bring in more cash.

Production machinery and equipment can be sold either all at once at an auction or piecemeal. Buyers of used production machinery and equipment consist of used-equipment dealers and private manufacturing companies needing specific pieces. The former normally buy at auctions, the latter by specific solicitation. Even in a down market selling individual pieces brings higher prices than auctions. An auction, however, will dispose of everything much quicker.

To conduct an auction you need an auctioneer and a location to hold the auction. The auctioneer handles the advertising to notify interested parties of the place and date of the auction and what specific pieces are included. Your company must pay for the advertising, all out-of-pocket expenses of the auctioneer, and the auctioneer's commission—normally 7 to 10 percent of the cash collected. Several reputable auction firms operate nationally. Check your local newspapers for advertisements or contact an asset-based lender. These banks can always recommend auctioneers they use at foreclosures.

Selling individual pieces of machinery and equipment takes more effort and time. One of the best ways is to ask a large used-machinery and equipment dealer to bid on one or more pieces. Names and addresses are listed in any metropolitan area yellow pages.

Placing advertisements in the "Equipment for Sale" section of your local newspaper also brings results. Some cities have regional advertising papers that don't charge for an ad until the item is sold. If you can locate one of these, by all means try it. With no charge until the sale culminates you can't go wrong.

The major difficulty with selling individual pieces of machinery and equipment is that you end up with a lot of strangers coming into the plant and disrupting personnel and production. Careful planning, however, minimizes this disruption.

The following summarizes the actions necessary to dispose of production machinery and equipment:

1. Take an inventory of all machinery and equipment.

2. Return any borrowed or unneeded leased pieces.

3. Investigate the benefits of holding an auction.

4. Contact used-equipment dealers for bids.

5. Run ads in the "Equipment for Sale" section of your newspaper or use special advertising papers.

Peddle Office Furniture, Fixtures, and Equipment

During tough times office furniture, fixtures, and equipment (FF&E) usually sells much faster than used production machinery and equipment. Good times or bad, it seems that people are always on the lookout for FF&E bargains. Individual pieces might not bring in as much cash as production machinery and equipment but at least the turnover is quicker.

Methods for selling used FF&E are about the same as with production pieces. Unless you have a large quantity, however, national auctioneers won't be interested. You'll have to go with smaller, local firms. Also, auction commissions on small sales can run much higher than normal—sometimes as much as one-third of the sale price.

Used office furniture and equipment dealers are a good source for a quick, inexpensive sale. Local dealers frequently offer a flat price for all the pieces and then they haul them away. Prices are normally very low, however—about one-tenth of replacement cost.

Most companies do much better selling FF&E piecemeal to individual buyers. Newspaper ads and advertising papers seem to work well.

If a company has used computers, printers, or peripheral equipment to sell, the Boston Computer Exchange (BCE) can be very helpful. This national chain brokers used computer equipment and also buys and sells for their own account. Prices are market competitive minus the BCE commission.

Local advertising papers and circulars also work well for disposing of computers. Annual introductions of modified computers and peripheral equipment by IBM, Apple, and other manufacturers coupled with the durability of these pieces has created a thriving national market in used computers. You should have no difficulty disposing of these assets and you'll probably be surprised at the good prices.

Steps for selling FF&E are:

1. Use an auctioneer for large quantities. Look out for unreasonable commissions.

2. Get bids from local used office equipment dealers. Beware of lowball prices.

3. Run ads in advertising papers or local newspaper.

4. Check with used-computer brokerages for help in this area.

Convert Cars to Cash

Everyone knows how to sell a car to a used-car dealer or through a newspaper advertisement. Prices are negotiated from market demand and the mechanics of the sale are relatively straightforward. Trucks and other road vehicles tend to be more difficult to dispose of, however, especially older vehicles. Newspaper ads work as well as anything. You might also try local auto repair shops. If they don't need the truck or other vehicle themselves, they might know of other businesses that do, as the owner of a rural lumberyard learned.

> Howard had owned the yard for over ten years. Although specializing in lumber for do-it-yourselfers, which frequently required home deliveries of small quantities, he also sold coal, sand, and gravel by the truckload. His trucks were so battered they brought nothing as trade-ins. Howard junked the first two. The third time around he offered the truck to a friend, P.K., who owned an auto repair shop. P.K. paid Howard $1,000 for the battered truck, fixed up the engine and transmission and sold it from his yard for $1,900. The two have since turned over four additional trucks too beat up to sell on the open market.

Forklifts, off-road vehicles, snowplows, trailers, electric carts, and other miscellaneous vehicles don't usually have much value. If you can get anything for them, the best source of buyers is other companies in your area. However, even if they can't be sold, at least junk them and get them off the premises. You can always use the space for something else—or lease it out.

Here's a listing of steps to follow.

1. Sell cars to used-car dealers or through newspaper ads.

2. Use newspaper ads for trucks and other road vehicles.

3. Try auto/truck repair shops as potential buyers for old vehicles.

4. Check with companies in your area as potential buyers of off-road vehicles.

5. If all else fails, sell them to a junk dealer.

Turn Dusty Inventory into Cash

Piles of production materials or stacks of unsold merchandise gathering dust don't generate cash. Markets can usually be found for unneeded materials or products regardless of how old they may be. If the items are battered, perhaps a distressed inventory sale will garner at least some cash.

Arranging a bulk sale to secondhand dealers is certainly the quickest way to dispose of old inventory. Special sale advertisements in a local newspaper also seems to work well for many types of businesses. Employees may be anxious to buy the goods if they are usable. If all else fails, sell to a junk dealer for any price you can get. Selling the merchandise at below cost might show a loss on your books but if you don't need the goods, cash in hand is better than inventory in the corner. In addition, losses are tax deductible so Uncle Sam actually makes up part of the difference.

Production and office supplies can also be included. Hardly any business is so efficient that it uses up all the odds and ends of its paper, cleaning solvent, computer printer ribbons, machine oil, lumber, and other leftover supplies. These products seldom wear out although they may be dirty or dog-eared. They are still usually worth something to somebody. Try selling to employees or other companies in your area. This usually works best for odd lots of supplies.

Spare parts for equipment you no longer have or for products you no longer sell can also bring cash. Customers that continue to use your old products may be more than willing to carry their own spare parts, especially if they can get them at a discount. Machine shops, distributors, repair businesses, and a variety of other companies that are in the business of fixing up equipment and machinery can probably use spare parts. If you can't find a buyer, try a yard sale—just like a garage sale to clean out your house.

In tough times the objective is to raise cash rather than sit on unneeded materials and parts. Any cash you can get is better than nothing. Even at 10 cents on the dollar you're better off cleaning house than storing the inventory for possible future use. By the time you get around to needing it again your business should be booming and you can afford to buy new items.

The starting point in cleaning up old inventory and supplies is to find out what you have on hand. Unfortunately, this means a physical inventory. Taking a physical inventory will most likely reveal parts, supplies, and materials you probably don't even know you own. So much the better. Surprise cash is as valuable as planned cash.

When I desperately needed to raise cash for a machine shop I ran several years ago, I asked my controller to make a list of all old inventory and supplies from his accounting records. The list totaled about three pages and I estimated the goods should bring in about $4,000 if we were lucky.

We took a physical inventory one Saturday expecting it to take about three hours. Monday morning we were still finding items that everyone had forgotten about long ago tucked away in corners, desks, storage closets, and in the basement of the building. We even located two old bicycles and a pair of skis.

This herculean effort resulted in extra cash of not $4,000, but $15,000!

The following summarizes methods to dispose of inventory:

1. Take a complete physical inventory of all materials, products, and supplies.

2. Sell unneeded materials and finished product to secondhand discount dealers.

3. Try newspaper ads for materials of value.

4. Ask employees to buy materials or products.

5. Hold a distress sale for battered inventory.

6. Sell useless inventory for junk to clear the space.

7. Include office and production supplies in each of these methods.

Squeeze Cash From Real Property

Obviously, selling the building that houses your business makes no sense unless you are liquidating the company. On the other hand, if you also own other property, this might be a good time to convert it to cash.

That garage you purchased to store unused equipment in won't be needed anymore once the equipment is sold. The below-market price you paid for that vacant lot down the street was a real bargain ten years ago and the property is probably worth much more now. If you ever do expand your facility, there will always be other land available. If your manufacturing plant consists of several buildings perhaps you can consolidate and free up one of them for sale. How about that old house you purchased a couple of years ago intending to remodel it for offices. You never did find the time to fix it up. Now is the time to cash in.

Just as with equipment and inventory, a bird in the hand is worth two in the bush. In tough times any property is more valuable as cash than it is sitting vacant or gathering dust.

If you are reticent to sell, why not consider leasing out unused property—buildings, land, even pieces of equipment. Frequently, leasing property brings in more cash than selling it. This is especially true of office or storage space. Leasing real property is like an annuity, the cash keeps rolling in year after year.

Even if the lessee files for bankruptcy and stops paying rent, as a lessor you still make out. One of the quirks in the bankruptcy code stipulates that lessors have preference over many other creditors and the court goes out of its way to make sure building rent gets paid.

Leasing out excess office space is another good way to raise extra cash. Over time, many businesses accumulate extra office space. Perhaps at one time extra space made sense for file storage, conference rooms, a place for the auditor to sit, special exercise rooms, segregated computer rooms, two or three executive offices for expansion, or an employees' lunch room. Are these conveniences really necessary now when cash is tight? Wouldn't it be better to convert this unnecessary space to cash by leasing it out? When lease periods end you can always reclaim the space if you really need it.

Company cars, extra personal computers or other office equipment, extra testing equipment, or a second forklift you had to have three years ago when your business was growing can also be converted to cash by leasing them out. Given a choice between losing their company car and leasing it from the company, most employees will opt for the latter. Holding on to extra computers expecting to add employees in the future is wasted money. Why not lease these to employees also? Most would probably love to have a computer at home. If you might need that spare forklift when business turns around you can always rent it out on a month-to-month lease and reclaim it when needed. The same principle holds for other production, testing, or support equipment.

It's usually a good idea to keep the lease period flexible, such as one year with optional renewals upon mutual agreement. A contract clause that allows cancellation with ninety-day written notice also adds flexibility. The idea is to keep property available for the next business upturn when you will probably use it again.

A summary of the steps for converting real property to cash is:

1. Sell nonessential property including garages, storage warehouses, vacant land, separate manufacturing buildings, and any other real estate not needed for survival.

2. Lease out extra storage, warehouse, or production space.

3. Find a tenant for unused office space.

4. Try leasing company cars and computer equipment to employees.

5. Rent extra production equipment and vehicles on a month-to-month lease.

Sale/Leaseback

Some businesses are eminently suitable to sale/leaseback arrangements. Hotels/motor inns, restaurants, health care centers, and fitness centers consistently use sale/leasebacks to conserve cash. Actually, any company that owns its own building (even with a mortgage) or any other hard assets can use sale/leaseback techniques to raise cash. You don't have to be a giant. Small businesses such as auto repair shops and contractors also benefit.

Sale/leasebacks are very simple to arrange. Lease agreements can be written for a building or an individual piece of equipment. Broad leases can also be written for groups of equipment with short useful lives, such as restaurant equipment, furniture and fixtures, and air conditioning systems. As one piece wears out and is replaced, the old equipment is deleted from the lease and the new piece added.

Originating a sales/leaseback requires finding a lessor willing to handle the type of assets you want to include and establishing a market price for the asset. Lessors abound. National companies such as Leaseamerica or General Electric Capital Corp. are eager to participate for larger, more expensive assets or groups of assets. Smaller, local or regional leasing companies can easily be contacted through the yellow pages. Any automobile dealer can point the direction to an appropriate leasing company that handles cars.

Establishing a market price can be a bit more difficult for some assets. Obviously, real estate appraisals can be obtained for real property and Blue Book values are available for cars. But what about a five-year-old air conditioning system? Or a set of office furniture? Or several computers and peripheral equipment from different manufacturers and of different ages? Market prices for these assets are usually taken from industry manuals similar to the automobile Blue Book. If such manuals exist, the leasing company will know where to find them. Recent market sales of similar used equipment is also a good measure. If all else fails, negotiate a price with the leasing company.

Lease periods for sale/leaseback deals vary. A lease covering one piece of equipment is usually based on the useful life of the equipment. Leases for groups of assets are arbitrarily set at three, five, seven, ten, or some other negotiated period. Building leases normally cannot be written for less than five years, and more likely seven to ten.

Obviously the benefit of sale/leasebacks is that an asset can be converted into immediate cash with a payback spread over a number of years, similar to a term loan from a bank. Except that with a sale/leaseback you end up with both the cash and the asset.

Sale/leaseback actions are summarized as follows:

1. Investigate sale/leaseback of buildings, production and office equipment, and vehicles.

2. Consider both types of leases for personal property—by the piece or as a group.

3. Use a national leasing company for large amounts and a local company from the yellow ages for small leases.

4. Establish a market value price.

5. Negotiate lease period to meet long-term objectives.

Consolidate Facilities

Another easy way to convert assets to cash is to consolidate facilities. If you have an office apart from your manufacturing plant, close it down and move into a corner of the plant. If you have two or more plants, consolidate operations in one location. Perhaps you sell nationally and have sales offices in two or more locations. Look at closing some or all of them. It costs less to have salespersons drive or fly to meet customers than to rent a separate office.

Perhaps you stock goods at one or more distribution warehouses. Why not consolidate everything in one location? If its centrally located, delivery and shipping costs are usually less expensive than maintaining a facility.

The same holds true for certain service businesses. Do you really need an office in Chicago and one in Rockford? Or one in downtown Washington and another one in Silver Spring? Owners of personal service businesses are notorious for shuttling back and forth between two or more offices. By more careful scheduling you can probably close down all but one and still service your customers/clients adequately. Tough times demand tough actions.

Sharing Office Space

Another way to convert space into cash is to share office space. This is just the reverse of a tactic reviewed earlier in this chapter. Instead of leasing out unused office space, move your office in with another company. If you are in a service business that does not require customer visits, banks are a good place to look for compatible office space.

Nearly all banks have overbuilt in the past ten years. Most are willing to rent out one or a set of offices, as long as your business doesn't conflict with bank business. Such space is usually less expensive than renting in an office building. Then you can either sell your existing office building (if you own it) or lease it out to another company, assuming you can get more than you have to pay the new landlord. If not, then obviously nothing has been saved.

Banks aren't the only good source of excess office space. Many hotels are more than willing to rent one or more rooms to be used as offices. In my area, all of the major hotels—Hilton, Holiday Inn, Marriott, Sheraton—rent out space as independent offices. Once again the rent is usually less than comparable office buildings. Of course customer visits to your office present no problem at all if you are located in a hotel.

Sharing space in smaller suburban shopping malls also works. Many times a store leases both the store front and second floor space for storage. In tough times one of these might be happy to rent you office space in the second floor area at very reasonable terms.

Switch from High-Rent to Low-Rent

While on the subject of renting offices, another viable way to convert space to cash is to relocate your offices from a high-rent district to lower-cost space. Is it really essential to the survival of your business that you have an office in midtown Manhattan, or on State Street, or Century City?

Such prestigious addresses are fine when business is booming but does an address create cash in tough times? For most businesses the answer must be no. I know it adds stature to a company to have a good address, but in tough times this public relations expenditure could probably be abandoned without much detrimental impact on sales.

A good friend owned a small advertising agency employing five people. For years he rented office space at a prestigious address in center city Philadelphia. When business slackened he looked for ideas to cut costs. I suggested moving the agency, including its personnel and equipment, to the suburbs to cut rental costs by at least one-third.

At first he resisted, arguing that clients expected an ad agency to have a first-class, center city address. Reason prevailed. He moved to the suburbs, found a location at less than half the price that he had been paying in center city, and his business actually picked up. He found more new clients in the suburbs in one year than he had added in three years in center city.

A prestigious location may be ego building, but is it really necessary for the survival of your business?

There are many ways to convert business assets to cash. We often ignore this valuable source of cash because we let our egos get in the way. After working for years to get a nice office, fancy company car, enough equipment to be flexible, and to invest in extra land and buildings, it's hard to turn the other way and recognize these luxuries for what they are. But in tough times you can't let your ego get in the way if you want to survive.

It's also easy to concentrate on cost reductions, and perhaps tactics to increase sales rather than the more mundane efforts required to sell or lease assets. Once again the ego bell rings. It makes good cocktail party conversation to tell your friends how you are tightening up your company with cost reductions. Making it lean and mean. It's even more fun to brag about sales tactics that bring in bigger market shares. But who wants to broadcast that they are selling off assets? This sounds too much like retrenching, even liquidation.

I have gone through this scenario with my own businesses. I know how great it feels when times are good and you're beating the hell out of your competition. What an ego builder it is to be considered a successful entrepreneur by your friends, neighbors, and competitors. I also know how bad it feels when prized assets must be sold off to stay in business. I'll never forget working for Harold Geneen in the heyday of ITT. His favorite motto was, "Never retrench, always build." But when tough times hit, it didn't work there any better than it works in small companies.

When times are tough there isn't any other choice. Cost cutting and sales promotions won't be enough. Eventually, everyone comes to the same conclusion. Face the music and strip the business bare. Raise cash anyway and every way you can. There is no alternative.

Chapter 9

Liquidity First

Restructuring Debt to Save Cash

Reducing costs, increasing sales, and selling noncritical business assets are essential recession-proofing actions. For some businesses those are the only available options to keep alive in tough times. For many other companies, however, a final piece to the recession-proofing puzzle must be put in place before you can rest secure that you've done everything possible to batten down the hatches. The fourth step is to reduce the amount of cash spent on debt payments.

In our credit-crazed society, borrowing money has become a way of life. We are all familiar with leveraging. We leverage in our personal lives by buying our homes with mortgage debt, buying our cars with installment loans, and charging purchases of necessary and luxury items alike to our credit cards. We also leverage our businesses by borrowing against receivables and inventory. We buy machinery and equipment with term loans. We buy company cars with installment loans. We buy plants, warehouse, and office buildings with mortgage debt. We even leverage the purchase of entire companies with an assortment of debt instruments.

For the past twenty years most of us have practiced the basic principle of using someone else's money to buy what we want and need right now and worry about paying for it later. This is the American way.

Borrowing huge sums of money for virtually any purpose may make sense in good times. Theoretically, as a business grows and creates more income it can pay back the borrowed money out of ever-increasing cash reserves.

But when business turns down and tough times hit, just the reverse occurs. Now you must pay back loans out of less cash reserves than you had when you borrowed the money. In tough times interest and principal payments easily become an overwhelming burden that drains cash needed for purchasing materials and meeting payrolls. Leveraging definitely does not make sense in tough times. A small business owner can make all the right recession-proofing moves and still not have enough cash to survive because every dollar gained goes to pay interest or principal on loans.

Before closing the book on actions to improve cash-flow, any intelligent business person must at least try to reduce debt service payments. This chapter highlights several ways to accomplish this seemingly herculean feat. Although you might not be able to use all of these suggestions, at least a few should help increase cash-flow in your business. We'll look at ways to reduce debt service payments (both interest and principal) under four headings.

1. Methods for reducing short-term debt (e.g., revolvers, lines of credit, credit card debt).

2. Ways to convert short-term to long-term debt to reduce monthly payments.

3. Ideas for deferring monthly debt service payments until times are better.

4. Suggestions for converting debt to equity shares of the business.

Get Rid of Short-Term Debt

The accounting fraternity defines short-term debt as any loan that must be paid back within one year. Typical short-term business debt consists of bank revolving lines of credit (revolvers), open lines of credit, promissory notes payable on demand, this year's payments against mortgages or other long-term loans, credit card balances, amounts due to suppliers, and income taxes. We have already looked at ideas for reducing income taxes. Chapter 12 offers suggestions for dealing with amounts owed to suppliers.

Short-term bank loans are the toughest to reduce. Revolving loans are the most difficult of all. Revolvers are borrowings against specific receivables and identifiable pieces of inventory that keep revolving from one week to the next. As you send out a billing invoice, rather than waiting for the customer to pay, you borrow 80 or 85 percent of the receivable from the bank. When the customer does pay, the collection pays off the loan, plus interest. The same principle holds for inventory loans.

Practically, however, banks don't make a new loan against every receivable account. Each day, week, or month, a company submits all of its invoices to the bank and the bank makes one loan at the agreed upon percentage of the invoices (80 or 85 percent normally). This system works fine on the way up, just as any leveraging scheme does. On the way down a business cycle, however, revolvers can be deadly. You are always paying back more than you sell so there is never enough to cover operating expenses. Anyone who has used a revolver knows exactly how devastating a downturn can be.

Open lines of credit are almost as tough to handle. In this case, however, instead of matching paybacks against invoices, you must come up with principal and interest payments due on demand notes—usually every thirty days. Once again, as business drops, cash available for debt service gets scarce and new borrowings are required to raise the funds to pay off old demand notes.

One of the best ways to resolve a short-term debt service crunch is to use part of the cash generated by cost-reductions, higher margins, or increased sales to pay off loan balances. Once you get the balances significantly below your borrowing base, a good portion of the cash generated from new sales can be used for operating needs rather than debt service.

The implementation of tighter collection procedures also brings cash in faster and this can be used to reduce short-term debt. The faster you pay down a revolver or line of credit, the less the impact high debt service payments make when business turns down.

Another alternative is to use the cash received from selling business assets to pay down short-term debt. This reduces the continuing payments and even though it uses up some or all of the cash you received from selling assets, it saves cash otherwise needed for debt service.

Convert Short- to Long-Term Debt

You don't save any cash over the long term by converting short- to long-term debt. In fact, you end up paying out more because the interest rate on long-term debt is normally higher. The advantage in making the shift, however, is that you push debt payments out into the future and thus conserve immediate cash. In tough times, every dollar saved here and now gives you more flexibility while waiting for business to pick up again.

As a first step, try negotiating with your bank to convert part or all of the short-term debt into a term loan. A term loan may be for two, three, four, or more years. Typically, the interest rate is higher than on short-term borrowings. You save cash, however, by scheduling monthly principal and interest payments that are much less than paying back the entire short-term loan. Cash is conserved in the same manner as it is with sale/leaseback arrangements. You keep most of the cash and pay back the loan, or lease, in small increments over time.

Another way that frequently works is to offer your bank additional loan collateral in exchange for extending the payment due date. Most banks are more than willing to accept such an offer because the more collateral they have the more they believe you are at their mercy, and the safer they feel. Examples of additional loan collateral might include:

1. A second mortgage on a company-owned building

2. Production machinery and equipment

3. Company-owned automobiles

4. On-road and off-road vehicles

5. Office equipment

6. Furniture and fixtures

7. Operative patents

Most banks are willing to take any business asset of value that isn't already used as collateral on a loan. Many are also willing to take a second position on assets already securing loans.

If you don't have the right type of business assets to satisfy the bank, you might have to pledge personal assets to get the bank to convert the loan to long-term status. Examples of personal assets banks love to have as security include:

1. A second mortgage on your home

2. Personal automobiles

3. Certificates of deposit and other cash-equivalent bank instruments

4. Life insurance policies

5. Mutual fund investments

6. Listed stocks and bonds

7. Pension entitlements

8. Valuable collector's items—stamps, coins, gold, etc

If you don't have enough personal assets to get the bank interested, personal guarantees usually work. Obviously personal guarantees make you liable for business debts. If your business can't pay, a personal guarantee allows the bank to sue you directly for any and all assets you may own to satisfy the loan. The same holds true for anyone else willing to co-sign with you (e.g., your spouse, a friend or relative, another business owner). I cannot recommend in good conscience that anyone allow a spouse or anyone else to co-sign a personal guarantee. The risk just isn't worth it. Better to search for a different way to solve your debt service problem.

Another method many business owners have successfully used to shift from short- to long-term debt is to shop the loan to different banks. In some areas of the country, notably in smaller communities, banks are not very competitive. They are a close-knit group and one bank will generally not compete directly with its neighbor for your business. In larger cities, however, a modest amount of bank competition does exist. It can't hurt to try. Maybe you can find a bank willing to grant a long-term loan with very little collateral.

To go this route following a few simple rules will nearly always net the best results.

1. Prepare a financing plan. Never approach a bank for a loan without a well-conceived financing plan. It should be typed, neatly packaged, and include sufficient market and product information about your business to allow the bank to quickly form a judgment. It should also include a recap of your personal background, and financial projections for your business. If you go this route, check out the full details of preparing financing plans in my book *When The Bank Says No! Creative Financing for Closely Held Businesses*. This book also presents a variety of ideas for raising money from sources other than banks.

2. Prepare a listing of the collateral you are willing to secure the loan with, including your estimate of the value of each asset.

3. Bring a personal financial statement listing the assets you personally own and the liabilities you personally owe.

4. Try to get your first appointment with a senior loan officer. He or she may shuffle you down the ladder, but it helps to start at the top.

5. If possible, carry a reference letter from your current bank. If that isn't possible, carry reference let-

ters from other bankers or financial professionals
you know.

6. Don't be disappointed if the first bank turns you
down. Keep trying other banks.

With the globalization of financing sources in the past few years,
a large number of foreign banks have opened offices in New
York, Washington, or Los Angeles. Many are already opening
branch offices around the country. If you can't swing a deal with
an American bank and one of these foreign banks has a branch
nearby, give it a whirl. Foreign banks seem to be far more competitive than their American counterparts. They are generally
eager to get new accounts—even small business accounts.
Foreign banks are also more creative in structuring financing arrangements than American banks. If you are short of collateral,
this might be the answer.

Another possibility for businesses with a significant amount
of hard assets—real property or machinery and equipment—is
to refinance with an asset-based lender (ABL). Asset-based
lenders evolved from the old industrial finance companies.
Some have become departments or divisions of commercial
banks. Others remain independent. They are listed in the yellow
pages under "Business Loans."

Asset-based lenders loan money on all business assets, but
many of them prefer term loans secured by hard assets. The interest rate is always more than that charged by commercial
banks, many times ranging from three to five points above the
prime rate. To offset this extra cost, most offer term loans of five
to seven years. You pay more over the long haul, but as a short-
term, recession-proofing tactic extending a loan due next month
to one due over a five-year period results in substantial cash
savings now.

Most asset-based lenders are fairly good business people
and they will try hard to understand your business before
granting a loan. On the other hand, you should be aware that
they are also tough to deal with if you start having trouble meeting debt service payments. Commercial banks don't like to

foreclose, but asset-based lenders are fully equipped to shut down your business and auction off the assets if you stumble.

If all else fails and you can't refinance short-term debt, it's probably time to try negotiating deferred payments with your existing bank.

Defer Debt Payments

During tough times, and especially in 1991, commercial banks have portfolios full of problem loans, many of them to small businesses. Commercial banks follow a basic principle: the most important item on their agenda is to get loans repaid in full. Income seems to be of secondary importance.

A second feature of commercial banks is that most of them, especially smaller banks, are not equipped to dispose of business assets on foreclosure. They do not maintain close contacts with auctioneers. They generally do not have problem-loan experts on their payroll to help a customer through the tough spots. In fact, this would be a conflict of interest and banks are usually careful not to be accused of interfering in a customer's business.

This lack of skills in collecting collateral coupled with the bank's primary objective to get the loan repaid, puts them in a vulnerable position. To your advantage, of course. The least-risk action a bank can take when you have a short-term cash crunch is to work with you and to try to get your business over the hurdle so you can eventually pay them back.

One popular way of achieving this is to grant deferred payments. Assume that you have a revolving line of credit that has fully absorbed your receivables borrowing base. Business slacks off temporarily and paying back the revolver is hurting your cash position.

If your banker would allow deferred payments on the revolver for six months, this would allow you to use collections to increase cash-flow. This extra cash could then be used to buy materials, meet payroll, and cover other operating expenses. Very frequently such a cash infusion is enough to get a business back on line. If you have been a good customer in the past, it's in the bank's interest to see you through. In most cases, granting deferred payments is the least-risk action from the bank's perspective.

Of course, the bank will probably insist that you continue to pay interest every month, but that's less painful than paying back the principal also. Many small business owners find this the least offensive way to restructure debt payments. And it can't hurt to ask.

I had a client whose business involved laying-up the fiberglass and the structural materials for sailboat and power boat hulls. All his jobs were done to customer specification for boat manufacturers. As manufacturers' sales of new boats declined, my client found his sales slipping as well. When his business was booming he used a revolving line of credit to finance his dated receivables. Now that new orders dropped off he was caught in a cash bind. He had nothing to ship, but his dated receivables were not due for another 150 days.

We approached his bank together with the proposition that the bank defer payment to a date six months after the dated receivables came in. This would allow my client to catch up on the payments against his supplier accounts and provide a partial cushion against the next dating program. The bank agreed. In addition, to tide him over, the bank agreed to an additional loan on a demand note for 150 days.

All banks aren't this generous, but if the bank can see that you will eventually make payment in full, it will usually grant the deferral.

Borrow from Nonbank Sources

If you can't seem to convince either your bank or a new bank to help, another recession-proofing method to raise extra cash is to borrow from friends or relatives.

I don't recommend this approach because I have learned the hard way over the years not to mix financial dealings with either friendship or family relations. It seems that friends and relatives love to give advice and verbal support. As soon as you ask for money, however, friends are no longer friendly and relatives get greedy. On the other hand, several clients have used these sources for short-term loans successfully. If the shoe fits, give it a try.

Other possibilities that have worked for raising short-term cash to pay off a revolver or an open line of credit are:

1. Short-term loans from suppliers

2. Short-term loans or advances from larger, continuing customers

3. Direct term loans or guarantees from the Small Business Administration (SBA)

4. Borrowings against a credit card line of credit

Converting short-term debt to longer-term payments might be the wrong approach to restructuring your debt. When times are tough exorbitant monthly debt service payments can hurt as much as paying back revolvers. If you find yourself in the position of fixed monthly payments to banks or other creditors and cost-reductions and sales tactics haven't created enough cash-flow, you are in good company.

Leveraged credit has been the downfall of thousands of small businesses in the past five years. With booming profits and easy bank credit it has been all too easy to jump at expansion opportunities without adequate cash reserves.

A new plant was easy to buy with 15 percent down payment and a twenty-year mortgage. Additional equipment seemed like a good idea, even if the purchase was financed with a ten-year term loan. New company cars could be easily financed with three-, four-, or five- year installment loans. Credit purchases of copiers, computers, fax machines, and other office equipment could easily be arranged through dealers and manufacturers. All it took was signing a five-year note.

The art of leveraged buying has been well-honed by purchasers and sellers alike. In 1990, of the $13 trillion of total outstanding debt in this country, the business sector accounted for more than one-fourth, or $3.4 trillion, just about equal to the outstanding debt of our federal government.

When times are booming people give short shrift to committing their business to cash-draining monthly debt payments. In tough times, however, the error comes home to roost. Unable to cope with debt loads, small businesses by the thousands are beating a path to bankruptcy courts.

If your business is saddled with monthly debt service payments that are eating away at your cash reserve, the balance of this chapter should help you generate a few ideas to get rid of debt completely, or to at least reduce it to a manageable level other than through the courts.

Exchange Debt for Cash and Business Interest

For many companies additional equity contributions is the last resort. When all else fails, it's possible to get friends, relatives, business associates, customers, or suppliers, to come up with enough cash to keep the business afloat. The smaller the business the more impact equity capital has on cash-flow, and generally the easier it is to locate sources of extra capital.

Adding equity can breathe new life into an otherwise dying business. If the amounts are sufficient, this may be the only cash injection needed to survive tough times. Of course, there is always a tradeoff. If outside equity can be raised, you must waive part interest in the business. For an owner accustomed to having it all to himself or herself, learning the hard way that shared ownership takes some of the thrill out of entrepreneurship can be a rude awakening.

Although selling a part ownership in your business is a drastic step that most small business owners refuse to consider, it does create extra cash. This extra cash can then be used to liquidate onerous debt loads. It is therefore a viable additional means to recession-proof your business.

Selling part ownership doesn't mean controlling interest. You still retain control of your company. Nor does it mean sharing management responsibilities. Selling ownership shares to someone who will interfere with your business would be foolish. The types of buyers that we'll be concerned with here are strictly investors. They are willing to give you cash in exchange for the possibility of earning some type of return on their money or of realizing significant appreciation in their investment, if and when you decide to sell the business or buy them out.

This chapter explores four possibilities for raising equity capital for small businesses. I have intentionally excluded methods commonly used by larger companies because these methods become too complex for many small business owners: working partners, limited partnerships, investment banks, venture capital funds, public issues, and so on. If you are interested in exploring any of these avenues, *When The Bank Says No!* should be must reading. The four equity raising sources we'll consider here are from customers, suppliers, friends or relatives, and employees.

Equity Cash from Customers
Many small businesses, but especially manufacturing companies, sell products to large as well as small customers. The larger the customer or the more important your company is as a critical source of supply, the higher the likelihood of attracting investment capital. Customers might also be willing to invest in your service business if the service you offer is unique, has a high sale value, and you have contracts or other assurances that you will continue to get paid for the service.

An example of the latter occurred with an artist who was commissioned by the owner of an office building to paint a mural on a lobby wall. Halfway through the painting, other commercial property owners liked what they saw. A large shopping center development company and three office building owners wanted to contract with the artist to paint murals on their premises over the next five years.

The artist wanted the work but didn't have enough money to buy the supplies, equipment, and pay for his living expenses for such large projects. The owner of the first building saw an investment opportunity and agreed to pay the artist $100,000 for a one-third interest in his business.

You don't have to be incorporated to attract capital from customers, although a corporation simplifies the mechanics. You don't have to have a large business to get investments from customers either. Frequently, the smaller the business the more attractive it becomes as an investment opportunity. The one critical ingredient, however, is that you sell a product or service that is either unique and valuable in and of itself, or that is a critical component of the customer's supply line.

The latter situation occurred with a machining company in which I was a part owner. We were the sole supplier of small turned titanium parts used in race car transmissions. Our major customer commanded 30 percent of this transmission market. As inflation pushed our costs to new highs, competition pounded our customer base and kept sell prices low. Our line of credit was at its maximum and we were still short of cash.

I warned this major customer that we needed to reduce our bank borrowings to provide operating flexibility. I also suggested that to safeguard his source of transmission parts he should consider buying 25 percent of our company. Two months later our short-term loans were paid off and we had $150,000 in cash reserves. The company is still supplying these vital transmission parts today.

An investment from a customer may not be a palatable alternative but it works in certain situations. Usually a supporting agreement stipulates buyout terms so you will have a way out when times improve.

The last thing any of us want is to be locked into specific customers for life. Economic and market conditions are dynamic, and as conditions change most companies need the flexibility to shift customers or product lines as needed to maximize market control. It's hard to do this when customers own part of your business.

Equity Cash from Suppliers

Equity investment from suppliers is usually easier to swallow. Properly structured, such an arrangement puts you in the driver's seat, not the supplier-investor. Why would a supplier be willing to invest in a small business customer? For many reasons, a few of which are:

1. In exchange for long overdue payments for purchases

2. As a method of tying up a customer for future sales

3. To lock out competition

4. For potential investment appreciation

5. To influence management decisions

6. As the first step in the eventual buyout of the entire company

7. For protecting sales to a valuable customer that is in financial difficulty

8. To forestall bank foreclosure or other interference with a customer's operations

You can create substantially more leverage to get equity capital from a supplier than you can from a customer, especially if the supplier is another small business. All you have to do is delay payments on account and blame the delay on shortages in cash-flow. It's done all the time during tough times, and there is very little a supplier can do about it short of cutting you off from future deliveries. But if you are suffering tough times, chances are the supplier is also. The last thing small suppliers can afford is to lose a good customer because of temporary cash-flow problems.

A neighbor owned a 50 percent share in a small bakery specializing in breakfast and dinner rolls, specialty breads, and a variety of bagels. The bakery did well for many years and was a landmark example of a profitable, well-run small business. My neighbor's partner decided to retire and a financial planner was engaged to structure a buyout arrangement to meet the estate planning objectives of both partners.

My neighbor agreed to buy out his partner with cash payments over a three-year period. He borrowed this cash from a bank on a promissory note secured by his house. Then tough times hit and bills piled up, including bills from the financial planner.

Seeing an opportunity for investment appreciation in the profitable business and also a chance to settle the outstanding account due him, the financial planner agreed to invest $25,000 in exchange for a 10 percent interest in the bakery. My neighbor used the money to pay off his bank note and the bakery went on to become a market leader in its area. As a footnote, the financial planner eventually recouped his investment with a ten-fold gain when my neighbor sold the bakery and retired.

Getting equity money from a supplier has become an accepted practice for many small businesses. In addition to liquidating onerous debt, such investments provide a means to be assured of continued supply of materials or continuing services at prices equal to or less than prevailing market prices. After all, the supplier-investor would reduce the market value of his investment if he overcharged.

Equity Cash from Friends and Relatives

Most of us have difficulty asking friends for money. Invariably, as soon as a friend lends you money he or she ceases to be a friend. It takes an unusual relationship to be able to mix friendship and business and retain the good qualities of both. Money has been and will probably continue to be a very personal matter. To admit to friends that you need to borrow from them to keep your business afloat tends to connote failure, weakness, and the inability to run your own affairs.

On the other hand, offering to sell a friend an interest in your business doesn't seem to have such a stigma. Even though the result is the same—you end up with cash to liquidate bank debt or to expand the business—an investment gives the impression of financial acumen from both parties to the deal. In certain types of businesses, a friend may not expect dividends or cash returns if he has the free use of your products or services. Such was the case with Joe Stienberg who owned a hotel in Florida.

> As a general practice, Joe leveraged everything he could in his hotel—room furnishings, restaurant and bar equipment, air conditioning and telephone systems, the hotel parking facility, and the hotel itself. He had very little of his own money in the

business and as long as room occupancy stayed at approximately 70 percent he made all his debt service payments and took out a substantial amount of money for himself.

When tough times hit and room occupancy dropped, Joe was in trouble. He had to find a way to pay off some of the loans. He approached his good friend and asked if Marty wanted to invest $500,000 in the hotel. The two friends closed the deal.

In exchange for his investment, Joe granted Marty the right to use any room in the hotel whenever he wanted, eat as many meals in his restaurant as Marty desired, and order any drinks from the bar that suited him. That was ten years ago. Marty still enjoys the free use of Joe's hotel.

Getting relatives to invest in a business is another matter entirely. If friends tend to give you the cold shoulder when asked for money, relatives can be downright obnoxious. Most family ties seem to be strong in every way except money deals. When I needed money to start my offshore foreign sales corporation (FSC) I couldn't interest one relative in loaning me start-up capital. Yet two friends made an investment and without their help I could never have started the business.

On the other hand, most families tend to stick together when a family member gets into serious trouble, even to the extent of giving up money. Many close-knit families don't wait for trouble to hit. They willingly assist regardless of the circumstances. It seems that in most cases, however, the level of family assistance lies someplace between these two extremes. It also seems that asking for investment money rather than a loan makes all the difference in the world.

The following five rules have helped many small business owners avoid family quarrels or misunderstandings when seeking investment capital from relatives:

1. Make the transaction formal. If you have a corporation, actually issue the stock certificates. If not, at least draft a simple agreement spelling out the ownership split.

2. Execute a written document spelling out when the investor will be paid off. Be sure you specify a get-

ting out date so the family investor knows that his or her money isn't lost forever.

3. Specify what return the investor will get—cash returns, appreciation, use of the business facilities or products, free services, and so on.

4. Try to structure the deal so that if the business incurs a tax loss the family investor gets the benefit of it on his or her personal tax return (e.g., an S corporation or limited partnership arrangement).

5. Ask for the minimum amount of money you need right now. Identify exactly what the money will be used for and then use it for that purpose.

When Martha needed extra cash in a hurry and couldn't get additional bank loans she learned the importance of this last rule.

Located in a small town in northeastern Pennsylvania, Martha's beauty shop had provided her with a comfortable, if somewhat spartan living for over ten years. Recessions are always tough, but Martha's town was located in an old coal-mining area that had been depressed for years. When the last recession hit, her beauty shop suffered more than a 60 percent drop in business. Although she cut as many costs as possible, and tried everything she could think of to increase sales, nothing worked.

Finally, as a last resort, she asked her brother-in-law in New York for a loan. He answered no, but said that he would consider buying a 25 percent interest in her business. Before investing the money, however, he wanted to know specifically how Martha intended to use it. The bother-in-law wanted to be absolutely certain it wouldn't be squandered. He didn't want his sister-in-law hitting him up again in six months.

Although hesitant to give up part ownership in her business, Martha finally acquiesced. She identified that she needed $18,000 to finance an advertising campaign, replace a worn out hairdryer, and to take up the slack in working capital from the sale of ten-set coupon books at a substantial discount. She got the money and it turned out to be enough. She is still in business. Even with only 75 percent of the profits, she reports that her lifestyle is better than ever before.

Equity Cash from Employees

If you have a number of employees, another alternative is to raise equity capital from them. Although not many employees are willing to invest their own money in an employer's business, this problem can be avoided by setting up an Employee Stock Ownership Plan (ESOP). Large companies have used ESOPs for years as an added employee benefit or as a substitute for wage increases during tough times. Business owners also use ESOPs to fund management buyouts when they are ready to retire. We are only interested here, however, in how ESOPs can be used to raise capital for liquidating debt.

Any corporation that has employees can set up an ESOP. You don't have to have 25 or 50 or 100 employees, or any specific number for that matter, to utilize an ESOP. Incorporated businesses of any size can qualify.

An ESOP requires a formal, written plan prepared in accordance with IRS regulations. Although some companies administer the plan themselves, it usually pays to leave this to a trustee; either a bank or other outsider willing to take on the job. Once the ESOP is functioning, it can borrow money from a bank or other financial institution specifically to purchase shares in your company. Since employees actually own the ESOP, this allows employees to acquire an ownership interest without using any of their own money. More important, it allows you to raise equity capital without going outside your company. This is how an ESOP works.

An ESOP is an employee profit-sharing plan created by the IRS. Your company contributes cash or other property to the plan either in lieu of, or in addition to, other employee benefit programs. The amount of contribution is irrelevant. It can be substantial or minimal. Regardless of the amount or form, contributions to the ESOP are tax deductible to your corporation.

As cash accumulates in the plan, the ESOP buys shares in the company. Although the ESOP actually owns the shares, the employees own the ESOP and are therefore the true beneficiaries. Obviously, as an employee benefit an ESOP is merely an IRS-endorsed tax gimmick. You could just as easily give the employees company stock, but if you did, this would be taxable income to the employees.

An employee benefit, however, is not the only use for an ESOP. In addition, an ESOP can be used to raise capital for the employees to purchase equity interests in the company. The ESOP gets its funds to do this by borrowing from a bank or other financial institution.

Lenders lean over backwards to finance ESOP acquisitions. The reason is simple. Only 50 percent of the interest earned by the bank is taxable income.

Before asking an attorney to draw up the paperwork for the plan it doesn't hurt to have at least a basic understanding of the IRS rules governing contributions to ESOPs, although they are rather convoluted. The following represent the most important features.

To qualify under the tax code, corporate contributions must be:

1. Paid in cash directly to the participants, OR,

2. Paid to the ESOP and subsequently distributed in cash to the participants within ninety days after the plan year ends, OR,

3. Used to repay an ESOP loan.

A few additional restrictions also apply:

1. The company contributions to the ESOP must be allocated to each of the participants' accounts, and this allocation must be made on the same basis as the pro rata share of each participants' annual compensation to the total compensation paid.

2. Compensation in excess of $100,000 per annum is excluded from this calculation.

3. All participants must have nonforfeitable rights.

4. Employer securities must remain in the ESOP for seven years, except for:

   a. death, disability, separation from service, or termination of the plan, in which

189

case securities may be withdrawn by the participant, or,

b. transfer of a participant's employment to an acquirer corporation, or,

c. disposition of the selling corporation's stock in a subsidiary when the participant continues employment with the subsidiary.

The ESOP is responsible for debt service payments on loans it takes to purchase equity interests. Your company is totally free of this liability. You don't have to be a tax expert to use an ESOP. Most small business owners are not. Just get a qualified tax attorney to handle the paperwork and you should be all right. Although ESOPs seem complicated, they are an excellent way to get additional equity cash into the business without asking customers, suppliers, friends, or relatives. In addition, after going through a stringent cost reduction program, employees should regard the establishment of an ESOP as a good omen that their jobs are safe.

Summary
This chapter has explored a variety of ways to restructure a company's debt load to conserve cash and to bring additional cash into the business. Hopefully, you won't have to use any of these methods. With a stringent cost-cutting program, with the implementation of protective marketing strategies, and with extra cash raised by selling unneeded business assets, you may be able to handle existing debt service. However, if these efforts don't provide enough extra cash-flow, you should consider debt restructuring.

The following summarizes the debt liquidation and restructuring ideas covered in this chapter:

1. Methods for reducing short-term debt.

a. Use part of the cash generated by cost-reductions or increasing sales to pay off loan balances.

b. Implement tighter collection procedures to bring in cash faster and reduce revolver lines of credit.

c. Use cash received from selling business assets to pay down short-term debt.

2. Methods to convert short-term to long-term debt to reduce monthly debt service payments.

a. Negotiate with your bank to convert part or all of the short-term debt into a term loan.

b. Offer the bank additional collateral in exchange for extending the due date of the loan.

c. Pledge personal assets as an incentive to the bank.

d. Offer personal guarantees as incentive.

e. Shop the loan to different banks.

f. Consider switching to a foreign bank.

g. Refinance with an asset-based lender.

3. Defer debt service payments (at least the principal payment).

4. Borrow from other sources to pay off bank loans.

a. Friends and relatives

b. Suppliers

c. Customers

d. SBA loans and guarantees

e. Credit card line of credit

5. Raise equity capital to liquidate debt from

    a. Customers

    b. Suppliers

    c. Friends

    d. Relatives

    e. Employees (through an ESOP)

Chapter 10

Short Of Help

Tips for Recession-Proofing Small Service Businesses

Recession-proofing a small service business takes ingenuity. By small, I mean a business run by one person, the owner. You may employ part-time secretarial, typing, or bookkeeping help, or you may need one full-time employee to run the office or to help with sales. Generally, however, the term applies to one-person businesses.

By service business I mean a company whose only product consists of one or more types of services performed by the owner.

A listing of the types of services falling into this category could take up the rest of this book. A few examples of typical owners of small service businesses are barbers, astrologers, artists, writers, bookkeepers, public accountants, physical therapists, literary agents, business agents, professional speakers, publicists, consultants, investments advisors, financial planners, counselors, therapists, manufacturers representatives, and freelance journalists.

Small service businesses have several common characteristics. They all require an office, lab, shop, or other location as a home office from which to operate. They all must keep records, for tax purposes if nothing else. They all incur business expenses: telephone, supplies, automobile, tools or equipment, bank charges, insurance, and so on. Most use advertising or public relations to obtain customers/clients.

In addition, all small service businesses have the same two recession-proofing problems: (1) how to cut costs when there isn't much to cut, and, (2) how to increase revenues (sales) without adding personnel. The second problem comes down to the question of how to perform work for customers/clients on the one hand, make marketing time to attract new customers/clients, and still have enough left over to handle administrative chores.

There are only so many hours in a day and a person can't be two places at once. You can't perform your service and at the same time promote new business and also manage administrative details. The fact that small service businesses function without employees and without goods or products to sell sets them apart from other companies when it's time to recession-proof.

Small service businesses face the same sales/cost problems in tough times as manufacturing, distribution, retail or larger service companies, but must employ solutions unique to their characteristics. This entire chapter is devoted to ideas and suggestions to help this large bloc of small business owners.

Cost-effective sales tactics usually involve arrangements with other business owners to share expenses of sales promotion activities and to help with marketing and administrative activities. By sharing these activities with other companies you can accomplish the same recession-proofing results as your larger counterparts.

Sharing the Work Load by Using Informal Partnerships, Consortiums, and Networks

If a therapist, writer, public accountant, manufacturer's representative, or other small business person can somehow get another person to share the workload, then there will be more time to handle administrative and marketing activities. Sharing helps each party reduce costs and increase revenues. It's always a win-win situation. Three of the most common methods for accomplishing this without losing your independence or identity as a separate business entity are by using informal partnerships, loose associations or consortiums, and networking.

Informal Partnerships

An informal partnership specifically does not refer to two or more parties entering into a partnership agreement under one business name. Nor does it connote two or more parties agreeing to share business liabilities, income, or expenses. An informal partnership is not a legal entity. No partnership tax returns are filed and no state or federal identification numbers are used. Each partner continues to operate as an independent, the same way you always have.

There is one major difference from being completely on your own, however. When you work on one of your partner's jobs or deal with one of your partner's clients or customers, you act under his or her company name, not your own. If you have a consulting business, for example, and you work on a project for a client of your partner, the client billing will go out under your partner's name, not yours. Payment will be made by the client to your partner. Your partner, in turn, reimburses you for work performed.

This sounds complicated but it really isn't. Informal partnerships exist in practically every small service industry. Most people don't know about them because the appearance is always that of a true partnership or an employer/employee relationship. Another way to look at it is that as an independent contractor you are selling your services to your partner. I work this way quite frequently when I am between major consulting engagements and have billable time to spare.

Last summer for example I had a free week and a friend, who is also a consultant and with whom I have an informal partnership, was overloaded. He asked for my help. I did a project for one of his local clients while he was on an out-of-town engagement. I wrote my report to my partner, who in turn transferred the report to his letterhead and sent it to the client, along with a billing for my hours.

The client paid my partner, and my partner paid me. I gained by picking up extra income during a down period. My partner gained by satisfying his client in a timely manner. The client gained by getting the job done when he wanted it done. Everyone was a winner.

Informal partnerships also work in reverse. For example,

> Mac Strong had a manufacturers rep business selling small hand tools. When the economy flattened out, Mac spent all week on the road trying to get existing customers to place bigger orders. He had no time remaining for telephone solicitations of new customers, which normally accounted for one-fourth of his time.
>
> Mac asked another rep, Bill Burns who handled a complementary line of tools and with whom Mac had an informal partnership, to help him out. Mac gave Bill a list of potential customers and phone numbers and Bill made the solicitation calls. Mac paid Bill for his time and effort and was able to cover his existing customers and continue his new account marketing efforts through his partner's efforts.

Informal partnerships do not have to be between businesses in the same line of work. Therapists and counselors, public accountants and consultants, investment advisors and financial planners, writers and publicists, business agents and manufacturers reps, are a few of the more popular combinations.

From an administrative perspective, informal partnerships must stay informal, without legal trappings. They must leave each partner free to handle his or her own business. On the other hand there should be some type of written document spelling out the relationship between the two parties. It should identify how various matters will be shared: billings, occupancy expenses, insurance programs, personnel, getting out positions, and so on. The agreement should be nonbinding, however. As soon as two independent entrepreneurs start trying to use the law to keep a partnership together, it inevitably falls apart.

Consortiums

Consortiums are another popular method for sharing work loads in certain types of small service businesses. A consortium is a temporary alliance of two or more business firms in a common venture. Consortiums work best when all participating parties are in similar businesses but each offers different services.

A good example of how a consortium works occurred between Marcia, who ran a computer service business specializing in installing local area networks (LANs); Fred, who sold and installed personal computer-based accounting software programs; and Anne who specialized in selling communications hardware and telecommunications software.

> Marcia booked an order to supply the hardware and install a LAN system at two hotels located on either side of a mid-size city. The customer wanted a complete accounting system installed on the LAN along with telecommunications capabilities between the two hotels and between the hotels, a centralized reservation service, and a large French corporation for direct reservations and billing.
>
> Marcia, Fred, and Anne had formed consortiums before for large jobs and already had the mechanics in place. Over a six-month period the three installed the hardware, communications equipment, and the software to the customers satisfaction. Upon completion of the project, each went their own way on other jobs. Without the consortium Marcia could not have booked such a complex order. With the consortium she increased her billings by $100,000 in six months.

Consortiums work great for small service businesses. It's a terrific way to increase sales, and hence cash-flow, by sharing technical skill specialties. In tough times, this is one of the fastest ways for small service businesses to increase sales and develop a public image as a quality company capable of handling large jobs as well as small. As a temporary alliance, consortiums can be formed without any formal agreement or legally binding contract. It's just a matter of searching out businesses that augment your specialty and informally agreeing to sell and perform complementary services together.

Networking
Networking is very similar to consortiums except that the identification of special firms included in the network is not used as a marketing tool. Only the diverse capabilities of each specialty are marketed. And they are marketed by each of the participating firms. Usually each firm offers a specialty different from each of the other businesses. The basic idea in networking is to

permit a small service business to offer customers a complete service capability without incurring payroll costs or the complexities of a partnership.

Networking is very popular with management consultants, physical and mental health care businesses, financial planning firms, bookkeeping and tax services, and general contracting. Each participant in a network advertises full service capability. When a job is landed calling for skills not resident in the person booking the order, he or she merely calls on one of the other specialists to perform the work. The customer can either be billed by each company performing work or by the single business that books the order, who then pays each participant.

Businesses serving a large regional or national market can use networking to share the workload in different parts of the country, thus reducing or eliminating travel expenses. In this case, networking becomes a referral service and the business booking the order gets a referral fee.

Regardless of which format is used, sharing workloads permits a business owner to increase sales and serve a larger market than he or she could possibly do individually. As earlier chapters pointed out, one of the major recession-proofing actions is to increase sales and profits while making minimum cash outlays. Informal partnerships, consortiums, and networking all serve this end for small service businesses.

Group Advertising and Sales Promotion Tactics

Another benefit of informal partnerships, consortiums, and networking is that the group can share advertising and sales promotion expenses without the danger of competition arising between group members. On the contrary, a united front often produces the image of a company as a much larger firm than it really is.

When competing in a market with larger firms, this can be crucial in a protective marketing strategy. A commercial artist trying to compete with large advertising firms has a difficult time controlling his or her market niche. A commercial artist with the ability to draw upon diverse talents of several other commercial artists stands a much better chance of winning jobs at least on a par with larger agencies.

Advertising and sales promotions get the point across to the market that you are no longer alone, a one-man band, with limited resources and work schedules. A comprehensive advertising campaign touting the virtues of the group conveys a strong support organization, varied talents, broad resources, and the ability to handle larger projects.

One of my clients was a general contractor specializing in developing residential communities, complete with roadways, sewage, electricity, and water service. Bob had no employees and a small office with an answering machine. His days were spent on the road, supervising construction jobs, searching out opportunistic development sites, and coordinating with municipal authorities and real estate agencies. Bob used an unusual technique for sharing the expense of advertising to substantiate his performance credentials and financial viability for development permits.

> Bob had three large highway billboards positioned on the three major roads leading in and out of his community. The billboards included a large picture of Bob, and three other men with a caption that read, "Five-Star Development Corporation. Large enough to handle any job. Small enough to promise personal attention. Call Bob, Ted, Johnny, or Mike, or our corporate office for details."
>
> Ted had a heating, ventilating, and air conditioning business, Johnny ran a carpentry and millwork business, and Mike was a master electrician. Each ran their own business. Each of the four businesses shared in the cost of the billboards. And each of the men had more business than they could handle.

A different approach was used by Chuck, a computer systems specialist from Los Angeles, when advertising the services of his consulting business.

> Recognizing that larger firms were getting the larger clients, Chuck established a network with ten other single consultants, public accountants, tax specialists, and lawyers located in Los Angeles and San Francisco. Each business contributed one-tenth of the advertising expense to prepare a two-page circular describing eighteen service specialties that the combined

group could handle. They mailed it to all companies in the Los Angeles and San Francisco areas that employed between 100 and 500 employees.

Within three months the revenues of each member of the group showed a significant increase. Chuck ended up with three large clients each of whom told Chuck they would not have hired him without the breadth of specialities offered by his partners.

Two problem areas seem the most bothersome when sharing advertising or promotion campaigns: deciding on the type of advertising to do and avoiding any conflict of interest. I have never seen an easy answer to the first problem. You just have to sit down with the group and try to iron out differences. The second problem is easier to deal with. Most conflict of interest situations have to do with how to price each service, how to bill the customer/client, and how to collect.

Pricing Tactics for Joint Sales

The pricing of services sold by members of a group depends to a large extent on whether the members share operating expenses or whether each runs his or her own business entirely separate from the others. Some pricing formulas are more appropriate when group members share office space, office expenses, and advertising and promotion costs. Others work better if you each run your own show without sharing costs.

There are four basic ways of establishing group prices for services and then handling billing and collections activities:

1. Each group member is completely independent, sets his or her own prices with customers, sends out separate invoices, and collects his or her own accounts.

2. The group establishes the price, bills the customer, and collects moneys under a "doing-business-as" (d/b/a) name.

3. One group member subcontracts work from another.

4. A single price is billed to the customer and then split between group members performing the service.

Pricing and billing customers under a single group name is a common practice in informal partnerships. As far as the customer is concerned there is one supplier to deal with and pay. The group has a bank account under this name and pays joint bills from the account. Each month, or some other period, excess cash is distributed to each group member on a prearranged formula.

In effect, each business owner acts as an independent contractor. If it appears that conflict of interest conditions will arise in any given project, the member abstains from that job. A mutually agreed upon retainage in the group bank account takes care of contingencies.

Small service businesses in the building trades frequently use subcontracting as a means of organizing a project. The customer sees one general contractor as the producer of services. The general contractor is responsible for customer acceptance of the final product, bills the customer, and collects the account.

With a subcontracting arrangement, group members get paid for their services from the prime contractor and never interface directly with the customer. This minimizes the possibility of a conflict of interest. Subcontracting is effective with either an informal partnership or a consortium.

Fee-splitting is a common pricing arrangement in consortiums and networking. Frequently, the business owner who originally sources the work, but doesn't perform any services, is entitled to a sourcing or finder's fee paid by the group member who performs the service. In other cases with two or more group members on a specific engagement, one billing goes to the customer but participating members split the collections between themselves. Many health-care technicians, writers, and publicists performing in group arrangements earn their income this way.

Assuming an equitable arrangement can be reached for setting prices, billing customers and splitting up the receipts, significant amounts of cash can be saved by sharing the expenses of operating a one- or two-person service business.

Sharing Operating Expenses

The expenses in a service business without employees occur either when selling your service or as administrative expenses just to keep the business running. Most sole proprietors also have personal expenses that are legitimately paid by the business and qualify as tax deductible business expenses.

Selling Expenses

In addition to the cost savings benefits of sharing advertising and sales promotion expenses, major selling related expenses might include:

☐ Automobile

☐ Sales literature

☐ Travel

☐ Entertainment

Ideally, all of these expenses can be reduced by sharing arrangements with other business owners. The beauty of sharing selling expenses is that it doesn't matter whether you share office space with anyone else or not. All of the suggestions for sharing selling expenses can be accomplished with another business owner, or owners, regardless of location. Let's take a look at some of the possibilities that others have used effectively.

As anyone who makes personal sales calls or who provides service at a customer's location knows, automobile expenses can easily get out of hand. Any action that reduces car expenses is beneficial. The three largest expenses seem to be the original cost of the car or lease payments, fuel, and insurance. There isn't much you can do about sharing repair costs, except tires, but ways do exist to cut the other expenses.

The first step should be to arrange with several other business owners to combine forces and lease cars under a fleet arrangement with a national leasing company. You don't need to put the cars into a separate company. As long as each individual is willing to enter into a lease and shares the responsibility for making the lease payments, nearly any major leasing company will handle the deal. Or you can go through a dealership leasing program.

Fleet leasing is always less expensive per car than a single lease. You don't even need to have the same type of cars. If you or your associates already have cars, a fleet sale/leaseback arrangement can be implemented with a double-barreled effect—it reduces the cost of leasing the car by yourself, and it provides extra cash right now.

If you go with a fleet lease, you should be able to insure all the cars under a fleet policy. Once again, properly chosen, fleet policies are normally less expensive than insuring each car individually. You can even vary the coverage for each car. Different deductibles, different liability, and different bells and whistles (e.g., towing).

Buying tires for all the cars through the same tire dealer should also net discounts. Maybe not much, but you should be able to negotiate a better price than on you own.

With the so-called oil crisis, service stations will probably be reluctant to offer any discount for volume purchases. On the other hand, it's possible. A few years ago four other business owners and myself negotiated a two cent discount for all our purchases from one station. Of course, we had to guarantee a minimum gallonage each quarter.

The cost of producing sales literature is a bit trickier to share. However, some of the costs of putting together price sheets, sales brochures, promotion circulars, and so on, can be reduced by sharing. The two biggest cost savings involve volume discounts. Small print shops are susceptible to negotiated discounts for promised volume over a period of time. Small advertising agencies can also be amenable to reduced rates if you all use the same agency.

Some travel agencies, especially those in smaller towns or ones just starting up will give discounts for airline tickets purchased in quantity. If you and other members of your group travel frequently by air you should be able to negotiate deals with a travel agent providing you all agree to buy your tickets at the same place.

Entertaining customers is another expense than can be shared—at least some of the expense. Several golf clubs, fitness gyms, tennis clubs, and so on offer discounts for bulk membership purchases. Sharing the cost of season tickets to professional or college sporting events can help. Some business owners have gone as far as purchasing a boat, lodge, or vacation cottage jointly for mutual use while entertaining customers. As with other expenses, it's usually less expensive to do something in volume, and entertaining expenses are no different.

Administrative Expenses
Sharing administrative expenses is usually easier than sharing selling expenses. Some of the major administrative expenses that can be reduced by sharing are:

- ☐ Office rent
- ☐ Electricity, water, fuel
- ☐ Office supplies
- ☐ Legal and accounting fees
- ☐ Dues
- ☐ Subscriptions
- ☐ Liability and property insurance

You don't need an informal partnership, consortium, or networking arrangement to reduce these expenses. The following tips can be implemented by anyone.

If you are renting your own space in an office building now, why not consider moving to one of the popular executive office suites? Renting space under one of these arrangements is a marvelous way to share several types of expenses with other business owners. The following describes how a typical executive office suite arrangement works.

Normally the suite will be in a first-class office building. It will have a lobby and a receptionist who doubles as a telephone operator. Secretarial services are provided either by the receptionist or by a full-time secretary. There might be four, five, six, or more single private offices, completely furnished with more than adequate desks, chairs, lamps, telephones, and so on. Most suites come carpeted and draped. The suite of offices will have an office equipment room with copying and facsimile machines. Some of the newer ones have now installed LAN computer systems.

These services are all shared by individual businesses that rent one or more of the private offices. Rents run higher than a single office without all the amenities, but by the time you consider all the expenses you have to incur to run any size office these higher rents look very reasonable. By selling your office furniture and fixtures, as reviewed in chapter 8, terminating any part-time secretarial help, stopping your telephone service, and eliminating charges for electricity, moving into one of these suites can result in a significant cost savings.

If an executive office suite doesn't appeal to you, there are other ways to reduce office costs. You might sell your copying and fax equipment for cash and use a quick-print shop as needed. Most of them have fax service as well as copying equipment. It's much less expensive using these facilities on a pay-as-you-go basis than owning the equipment yourself.

If you can't get by without instant access to copying and fax equipment, why not structure a sale/leaseback arrangement with a used-office equipment company? Try the same approach for personal computers and peripheral equipment.

If you have an extra office, or room for an extra desk why not rent it out to another one-person business? By sharing your office, you not only raise extra cash from rent, you can also share the cost of office supplies, utilities, and telephones.

Do you really need all those magazine and newspaper subscriptions? Get other offices on your floor to share magazines and newspapers with you. You subscribe to one and pass it around. Someone else subscribes to a different one and passes it around. A third business takes the *Wall Street Journal* and passes it. Everyone doesn't need to pay for the same magazines and papers.

Do you really have to belong to four professional organizations? Why don't you pick one and ask each member of your group to choose a different one? That way you can share the information from several trade groups without spending all the money on dues.

Property insurance is another cost that can be shared. If you have several businesses in your office or adjacent offices, or if you use an executive office suite, all the businesses can join together and take one policy covering all their equipment and supplies inventory. Liability insurance for most businesses can also be shared. This time with other members of a trade group. Many trade associations now offer discounted liability insurance for members and you might as well take advantage of it.

Following are a few other ideas for sharing or otherwise reducing administrative expenses:

1. Buy generic brands of computer printer ribbons and computer paper.

2. Use the backs of computer printouts for scratch paper instead of paper pads.

3. Buy a space heater and keep the thermostat down.

4. Buy a fan and keep the air conditioning turned down or off.

5. Sell all furniture and office equipment not crucial to survival (see chapter 8).

6. Sell computer time to local schools for student training.

7. Eliminate call forwarding, touch tone service, inside wire maintenance contracts, and other telephone company services you really don't need.

8. Take a hard look at your telephone system. Can you get by with less equipment?

9. Convert your personal computers to leases through a sale/leaseback.

10. Sell your office furniture and lease new furniture, carpets, drapes, from an office furniture leasing company.

Tactics for Cutting Personal Expenses
Small service business owners frequently pay too much for their health and life insurance because they are not aware of new group policies specifically designed for sole proprietors. A number of insurance carriers now offer small business group rates for a single person company. Local trade groups also offer group coverage. As do some chambers of commerce. Look around. Chances are good that you can get better coverage than you now have through small group rates.

You also might consider dropping some health insurance coverage to reduce costs. Is it really necessary to get reimbursed for routine visits to doctor's offices or dentists? Can you afford to pay the first $500, $1,000, or $5,000 of insurance costs yourself? If you can, many small group policies now offer major medical coverage with high deductibles—up to $20,000—at much reduced rates.

Life insurance also bears a second look. Every year new forms of term policies arise as brainchilds of competitive insurance companies. These promotional policies can substantially reduce life insurance premiums, assuming you are in good health. If not, obviously hang on to what you have.

Many personal expenses of sole proprietors can be deducted for tax purposes if structured properly. It would probably pay to spend some time with a qualified tax accountant or attorney to find out what you can legitimately deduct. Don't go just by Sylvia Porter, tax newsletters, or articles from the daily newspapers. Every dollar of taxes saved is another dollar you can use to run the business. Tax savings are as good a cost reduction as anything else.

While we're on taxes let's take a look at one of the biggest administrative cost reductions available to small service business owners.

Benefit from an Office in the Home
Certain types of small service businesses must be conducted out of formal offices with all the trimmings. If you have many customer/clients visiting your office you obviously want it to be convenient and look classy.

On the other hand, many business owners never see a client or customer in their office. Business is conducted by phone, at the customer's office, or at an independent location. Bookkeepers, freelance journalists, writers, artists, consultants, and many other service business owners never have customers come to their office. In that case, get some real cost savings by closing down your office and opening one in your home. Even if clients/customers do come to your office, if your have the right surroundings at home, you can service them there as well as in a rented office.

Charles ran a successful therapist business for ten years in a fancy, midtown office in San Francisco. The continual increases in rent, parking, and utilities forced Charles to reassess the need to be located where he was. He decided that since most of his clients came from suburbs located north of the city and since he also lived across the bay in San Rafael, it made sense to open an office in his house. He did, and instead of losing business, he soon had more clients than he could handle. Many told Charles they would rather come to a local therapist than drive all the way into the city.

The Tax Reform Act of 1986 severely restricted business deductions allowed for maintaining an office at home. However, court cases in 1990 have loosened up these restrictions. Once again an office in the home can save significant taxes as well as reducing cash expenditures. This is a terrific way to cut business costs and reduce taxes simultaneously.

Assuming you meet the IRS Code qualifications for having a business office in your home, and nearly all small service business owners do, it's pretty hard to beat this cost reduction. Following are the major personal expenses you can take as business deductions with an office in your home. Of course, all are apportioned to the space you use in relation to the total space of the home.

1. Electricity, water, fuel

2. Personal telephone

3. Trash removal

4. Yard cleanup and maintenance

5. Home insurance

6. Repairs to the home, furnace, electrical or plumbing systems

7. Depreciation of your home

8. Condo fees

None of these expenses are deductible without an office in your home.

In addition to these personal expenses, you can deduct proportionate shares of property taxes and mortgage interest (the balance of both can be deducted as personal deductions). And of course you can still deduct the normal business expenses of travel, office supplies, telephone, and so on directly attributable to your business.

Taxes
Although this is certainly not a tax book and there are too many variations in the tax code to even touch the subject here, any one running his or her own business must be aware of the enormous number of legal tax gimmicks available to private businesses. They range all the way from tax deductions for the tuition you pay for your son or daughter at college to reducing tax rates by spreading income to your spouse and children to salting away tax free dollars for your retirement years.

If you would like to see how these and other tax related strategies can be legally used to reduce your tax burden, and therefore increase your business's cash-flow, pick up my book *Tap The Hidden Wealth In Your Business: Use Your Closely Held Company to Increase Personal Cash, Maximize Retirement Income, Build Estate Assets . . . All Legally!*

With federal and state taxes taking such a large bite out of your business cash—and whether you pay 15 percent, 28 percent, or 34 percent, that's a lot of cash going out the door—it behooves everyone, and especially small service business owners, to make every effort to minimize taxes.

The best starting point is a competent, tax advisor—either a CPA or a tax attorney. This is one place you should not try to cut corners. Taxes account for too much of your cash to trust advice from anyone but an expert. Stay away from tax services and others who are not expert in business taxes. They may be able to prepare your individual tax return, but don't trust them to plan for minimizing taxes from your business. Spend the money and hire an expert.

Chapter 11

When Your Market Shrinks Don't Stand Still

Recovery Strategies for Changing Markets

In tough times markets change. You can make all the right moves and still lose the race if someone alters the course. That's exactly what happens in many markets when competition stiffens, materials become scare, government regulations force untenable compliance requirements, or new technology makes products and processes obsolete. Being caught in markets experiencing one or more of these uncontrollable circumstances usually means either the end or the radical contraction of your business unless new markets can be opened.

In the past few years we've seen the collapse of the junk bond market obliterate high-flying leveraged buyouts. Companies specializing in this market have either folded (e.g., Drexel Burnham Lambert) or shifted gears to different markets (e.g., Prudential Bache). Small investment banks, securities dealers, and investment advisors have been hit even harder.

We've seen massive cuts in federal defense spending knock hundreds of small subcontractors out of the government contracting business. Either they have adapted to new markets and products or they are out of business.

Real estate developers, large and small, have closed their doors or changed their strategies in the face of plunging real estate markets. The introduction of compact disc recordings has bludgeoned both the LP record producers and manufacturers of LP record players. And on it goes.

When markets change, large companies usually have the resources to convert product lines or divert sales efforts to new markets. Small businesses aren't always that fortunate. For them, creative new marketing and product strategies must take the place of massive cash outlays. This chapter presents ideas for developing such strategies to enter new markets that afford a reasonable opportunity for survival and growth.

The key to identifying new, recession-proof markets is called selective market penetration. The underlying strategy in employing selective market penetration is to choose those markets with high demand and meager or ineffective competition.

Selective Market Penetration

Most of us become wedded to specific markets for our products or services simply because we have sold into these same markets for years. We tend to accept our competitive position as fixed, unchangeable, not susceptible to improvement. Entering alternative markets strikes fear in our hearts. Continuing to do what we have always done lends a sense of comfort and security. Only when we see these markets falling apart, when our major customers turn to other products, or competition offers better quality, lower-priced products or services, do we recognize the need to change. We then hustle to attract new markets or introduce new products. Often the effort is too little, too late.

Aggressive marketers continually search for new market niches for their products or services. They don't wait for competition to overtake them. At the first sign of weakening demand, they seek out new methods of selling, introduce new products or services, attract new breeds of customers, change distribution channels. Aggressive marketers constantly look for new market niches crossing the horizon that competition either doesn't see or is slow to enter.

As discussed in chapter 5, gaining controlling share of your markets is one of the most effective recession-proofing methods for protective marketing. This doesn't mean you have to sell more than 50 percent of the products or customers in a market.

You might have controlling share at 5 percent if there are ninety competitors with 1 percent or 2 percent shares. Regardless of the percentage, as long as you have the controlling share, you can manage prices, influence quality standards, and determine distribution policies. When identifying new markets, it's necessary to weigh the advantages and risks of entry against the probability of obtaining quick control.

A perfect example occurred when a client who serviced computer mainframes implemented an aggressive marketing strategy to enter a new market niche in order to counteract competitors' price cutting tactics.

> Jim Bludget ran a small computer repair service in the Midwest. He employed eight field service engineers to perform monthly maintenance and emergency repair services for local IBM and Honeywell mainframe computer users. Faced with intense competition from the computer manufacturers and several independent service giants trying to gain increased market share by discounting hourly rates, Jim decided he better make some changes or he would be out of business.
>
> Personal computers that cloned the popular IBM-XT model were just beginning to proliferate the market. Major computer repair companies shunned these machines as minor market entries that would soon fade away. Jim saw otherwise. He retrained four service engineers to handle these new machines and with a creative advertising campaign managed to capture the lion's share of this burgeoning market niche in his area. This enabled Jim to control his hourly rates and substantially increase margins. Four years later the company had quintupled its sales volume and increased its profits tenfold. Jim sold out and retired a wealthy man.

Identifying new markets or market niches that competitors haven't already penetrated is not easy. Too many of us faced with the daily struggles of running our businesses don't make the time to keep abreast of new technologies or changing distribution patterns that affect our products or services. Few of us recognize shifts in customer demand until more aggressive competitors have already established a beachhead.

Occasionally we read or hear about mergers, business acquisitions, or bankruptcies of major customers that inevitably push new competitors into our markets or make market niches we thought secure obsolete. But the press of business keeps us immobilized from snaring these new opportunities.

Yet, it is these shifting tides in the marketplace that produce new customer demands for products, services, pricing, and distribution, and result in the creation of new market niches. To implement selective market penetration actions, take the time and make the effort to remain cognizant of events occurring not only in the markets you currently serve but in other product lines and regions as well.

Several times in my own manufacturing and service companies I was faced with playing catch-up to competitors. New market niches arose. Before I took the time to intelligently assess if my company could grab a significant share, competition beat me to the punch. Eventually I zeroed in on a simple method for quickly assessing whether or not I should spend further time researching the likelihood of success in a new market. If the answer was yes to five of the following nine questions, the market was worthy of immediate investigation.

Criteria To Investigate New Market

1. Can I sell existing product lines or easily modified products to this market?

2. Will the market demand increase in the next twelve months?

3. Does the existing distribution system handle this market or can inexpensive variations be implemented in a month?

4. How much advertising or promotion will it take to get established and can this be done within three months?

5. Can the existing sales force sell to this market?

6. Is the market large enough and is demand strong enough to attract large competitors quickly, or can I establish a foothold first?

7. Is pricing based on market demand rather than cost?

8. Will technological change make my product line obsolete within two years?

9. Does after-sale service fit with my existing abilities?

If the answers indicated that I should take a look at this market I would then estimate how much cash was required for advertising, promotion, selling expenses, and product modification to make a strong entrance. If less than $10,000 I would jump at it; up to $25,000 I'd take a serious look; more than $50,000 told me to walk away.

And as globalization blossoms, global markets must be added to the list of potential opportunities.

Develop New Markets with Unique Advertising and Promotion Strategies

Assessing the potential for entering a new market can be a frightful task. If the new market characteristics differ radically from those currently served, it's worse. Unfamiliar customer demands, strange distribution requirements, hidden competition, and divergent pricing policies combine to block out newcomers. Advertising provides the key to open the door.

Chapter 6 reviewed the use of return coupons as a way to stimulate market interest in your product lines. Return coupons can also be an effective tool for testing new markets and for developing a new customer base.

Choosing an appropriate media depends on what you are trying to accomplish: introducing a new product, soliciting new customers, expanding into a new location, or any other approach to testing or developing new markets. The same approaches for attracting attention as mentioned in chapter 6 apply here.

☐ Direct mailings with return post cards

- ☐ Newspaper and magazine advertisements with a cut-out form

- ☐ Television spot commercials with an 800 phone number

- ☐ Trade shows and convention booths with mail-back handouts

- ☐ Trade show booths with registration forms

The choice of media also depends on how broad a market you are going after and how industry-sensitive it is. Local markets can be reached cost-effectively with television spots on local channels. Local newspaper ads are also effective for some products. Direct mail can be a cost-effective way to reach national markets. Certain trade shows focus on industry attendees, such as the New York toy show. Other trade shows are directed toward consumers, such as various home and boat shows around the country.

Regardless of the media, the success of using cost-effective advertising to test or penetrate new markets depends on the attractiveness and clarity of advertising copy. I paid substantial sums to learn this lesson when I started up my offshore foreign sales corporation management company.

Two investors lived in the Philadelphia area. One of them offered to assist in attracting new customers needing the services of an FSC management company. I decided to test the market by sending out a direct mail circular with a clip-out coupon. Trying to save money I prepared the copy myself. I quickly learned that one reply out of 500 mailings was hardly worth the postage.

The second time around I hired a small advertising agency to prepare the copy and artwork for a four-page, foldout sales brochure. The brochure included a return form to request additional information. This time we received more than 50 inquiries out of a mailing of 500 brochures. Obviously, the first mailing didn't attract much attention and was definitely not cost effective. The second mailing was very cost effective.

Promotional schemes also seem to work well for certain businesses as a way to test and open new markets. Contests and give away programs work well for small businesses selling new products. Offers of free installation can be effective when testing markets for various types of equipment. Half-price service offers can help attract customers when opening a new location for a service-oriented business.

Large corporations use promotional schemes all the time to promote new products or open new geographic or demographic markets. In 1990, AT&T wanted to get into the credit card business, much to the consternation of the banking industry. The company offered a substantial line of credit and no annual service fee to its existing customer base. The results were overwhelming and AT&T is now very much a factor in the credit card business. Sears used the same techniques several years ago when introducing their Discover card.

Obviously no single media, copy approach, or promotional tactic works for every business. Each must be customized to meet marketing objectives and market conditions. Nevertheless, to test or open a new market, some type of advertising or promotional technique will probably be necessary. As chapter 6 pointed out, as long as advertising and public relations efforts are intelligently matched to market objectives and applied with stringent cost controls they should be effective in increasing sales. The same holds true for using these techniques to test and open new markets.

The key is to be certain that the program matches your specific objectives and that you control the cost of the program personally. Results may not be seen for many months and during that period advertising costs can easily get out of control. Most owners find that advertising is not an activity that can be delegated. In small businesses, structuring an advertising campaign is too personal, its cost too high, and the results too uncertain, to assign this responsibility to anyone else.

Jump on the Global Bandwagon

Don't be afraid of looking at global (international) markets. With the exception of a few small service businesses restricted to local markets because of limited personnel, every company of virtually any size has the ability to compete in global markets. An extended list of resources and assistance stands ready to give you the tools. New customers demanding new products and services all over the world clamor for American companies to service these needs.

If your industry or the markets you presently serve are contracting, global markets of every size and shape present unparalleled opportunities for new entrants. In many cases you don't even have to modify your product line. Chrome furniture is as much or more in demand in Latin America than it is in this country. Markets for the same plastic toys sold in this country are mushrooming in Eastern Europe and parts of Asia. Steel pipe, iron forgings, and digital telephone equipment may be dying markets in America but are in high demand in many Third World countries.

Investment bankers and security analysts find a radically shrinking customer base in this country but such services are in high demand in Europe, Taiwan, Singapore, and very soon in the Soviet Union. Small real estate development contractors are finding work scare in the United States but demand for construction projects of all sizes and shapes is booming overseas—from hotels to power plants, from hospitals to schools, from roadways to airports.

Machine shops losing out as defense spending winds down can find an enormous demand for machined spare parts for aircraft, military equipment, ammunition, and a vast array of other uses throughout the world.

When tough times hit your markets in this country the only condition prohibiting you from searching out replacement markets overseas is a lack of information about when, where, and how to penetrate these burgeoning markets.

My book *Going Global: New Opportunities for Growing Companies to Compete in World Markets,* lays out a complete program for getting started in global markets. Because the subject is so broad, the best we can do in this chapter is to review a few of the most important aspects to consider.

Open New Markets through Exporting

For manufacturing and distribution companies, exporting is as good a place as any to penetrate selective new overseas markets. Aside from burgeoning customer demand and reduced competition, exporting presents several attractive features as an alternative to entering new domestic markets.

1. Overseas customers are easily identified by using worldwide sales representation networks already in place and through federal government sources.

2. Exporting absorbs a minimum of personnel resources.

3. Total financing packages can be obtained through the federal government, private sources, and major banks.

4. Chances are high that your existing product lines can be sold without any modification.

5. You can get paid by the customer at the same time you ship the products.

6. Prices are substantially higher than in declining markets in this country.

7. Specialized export firms stand ready to handle all the paperwork, shipping peculiarities, and insurance headaches, and their charges are built into product pricing.

Marketing and Administrative Assistance

Export management companies (EMC) serve three major functions for the small business wishing to broader its markets through exporting. EMCs are located in nearly every major city. Some have a full complement of twenty to fifty personnel. Others operate small businesses like yourself with five to ten people.

EMCs can act as your marketing department overseas through their worldwide networks of independent sales representatives and distributors. For a small fee, usually under $1,000, and a handful of your sales brochures, an EMC will solicit its sales network to determine in which country demand exists for your products. Local sales representatives will also advise what competition is already there, and what the prospects may be for developing your line.

EMCs also perform sales activities. Their sales reps book orders for you or accumulate customer inquires. They verify the credit worthiness of customers you choose to sell to. These are commissioned sales people and their commissions can be built into the product price.

At your request EMCs will handle all shipping documentation including arranging for ocean transport, preparing paperwork, and presenting documents for collection. You don't even have to leave your office if you don't want to. All charges for these services can also be included in product pricing.

If you would prefer, some EMCs act as brokers on their own account. They actually buy products and then resell them in world markets. It's just like selling domestically. In this case, however, the prices they are willing to pay for your products are substantially less than current market demand. After all, the EMC must make a profit also.

Of course, you don't have to use an EMC. You can contract with overseas sales representatives yourself. You can also handle all the shipping and collecting paperwork. It's much easier, however, and in the long run less expensive, to let EMCs carry the ball. At least until you become familiar with exporting protocol.

Financing Export Sales

Financing export sales is nearly always easier and less expensive than financing domestic production. The Export Import Bank (EXIMBANK), a federal agency, offers an array of financing options depending on the type of product you sell, the destination of the customers, and the types of customer.

Although EXIMBANK does offer direct financing to exporters, the most common form of financing assistance is guarantees to your local bank. With an EXIMBANK guarantee, most banks willingly lend working capital money to produce the products and also assist in financing the buyer of your goods.

With the active assistance of EXIMBANK, and through EXIMBANK other federal agencies such as the SBA, financing export sales is a snap compared to borrowing from a bank for domestic uses.

Collecting from Overseas Customers

A legitimate fear raised by small businesses thinking about entering export markets is how they can be sure of getting paid from a foreign customer. It's hard enough collecting domestically. The risk of foreign expropriation or a foreign customer not paying is just too great. Once you look into exporting, however, you will find that the risk of not getting paid is practically nonexistent.

For a modest charge, the Federal Credit Insurance Agency (FCIA), insures export shipments against all political and commercial risk. If the customer doesn't pay or if a foreign government expropriates your shipment, FCIA pays you.

But there is an even better way to collect against export sales: with letters of credit (LC). Nearly all small businesses use LCs for export transactions. An LC is merely a guarantee from the customer's bank to your bank, and therefore to you, that the amounts will be paid on time. A confirmed LC means that your U.S. bank stands behind the promise. Even if your customer's bank reneges, you still get paid. An irrevocable LC means that once it is placed, the customer cannot alter it in any way.

Although there are many variations of LCs, the most common form is an irrevocable, confirmed LC from your customer before you ship the goods, and in fact before you even begin production of the products. The LC calls for payment in full as soon as the goods are loaded on the boat. You get a bill of lading from the vessel's captain, present it to your bank, and return home with the cash in your pocket. Of course an EMC can do all this for you if you wish.

Between the FCIA and letters of credit, collecting from export customers is much easier, more certain, and much faster than collecting domestic accounts.

Once they master exporting, many business owners find that to really take advantage of new global markets they need to establish a sales office, warehouse, or even a manufacturing plant overseas. Once again, a plethora of financing, marketing, and technical assistance is available from the federal government and private agencies. There are far too many variations to cover in a book of this scope but if this idea seems appealing pick up *Going Global* to get all the details.

As pointed out earlier in this section, exporting applies principally to manufacturing and distribution businesses. Certain types of service businesses and construction companies can also use global markets as a recession-proofing strategy when local markets shrink.

Booming Global Markets for Service Businesses

Service businesses have a more difficult time expanding into global markets but that doesn't make the strategy any less appropriate. It just takes more ingenuity to accomplish. Global markets are clearly not applicable to the type of small service businesses that are the subject of chapter 10. It's impossible to service customer/clients in Germany at the same time you are doing it in New York or Chicago. However, slightly larger service businesses are finding foreign markets especially attractive in light of a shrinking domestic customer base.

A few examples of service businesses ideally suited to selective market penetration overseas include the following:

1. Repairing and maintaining office equipment and computers

2. Telephone answering

3. Management and engineering consulting

4. Professional—public accounting, legal, health care, architectural design, and so on

5. Installing and maintaining communications equipment

6. Laundry and dry cleaning (in certain countries)

7. Hotel management

8. Telephone marketing (in certain countries)

9. Financial services of all types

10. Water, air, and land pollution analysis

11. Waste management

Service businesses face a different set of problems overseas than do manufacturers or distributors. The biggest headache is a different language. If you are going to sell a service you have to be able to speak the buyer's language, especially when negotiating a contract. Thankfully, qualified interpreters are available to business people in most countries. Don't hesitate to use one.

Cultural differences can also cause confusion. Business protocol varies from region to region. Legal problems and licensing restrictions create hurdles. Many service business owners have overcome these obstacles, however, and if someone else can do it so can you.

While performing a business acquisition engagement in England, the owner of a commercial photography studio asked me for some help in getting established in Mexico. It seems that the British have as much difficulty expanding overseas as American firms. On returning to the U.S., I did a country survey of several locations the photographer was interested in on the east coast of Mexico. I didn't speak Spanish, had never done business in Mexico before, and couldn't locate the one business contact I knew in Mexico City. Three weeks later I beat a path to London and told the photographer that if he really wanted to open a studio in Mexico he should accompany me on the next trip.

The following month we joined forces in Mexico City, made licensing arrangements, hired an attorney, and set out for the east coast. It took three weeks, but we finally negotiated a contract for the rental of a studio, purchased office furniture and a few pieces of photography equipment, and hired a secretary and a sales manager—all through an interpreter. Eventually, my client overcame cultural shock and today has three thriving studios in London, Veracruz, and San Pedro Sula, Honduras.

After more than two decades of engaging in global business I strongly recommend giving the global community a try, especially if your domestic markets are shrinking. I also suggest the following guidelines that always seem to help clients just getting started in a foreign country.

1. Don't hesitate to hire an interpreter.

2. Clarify every word of every negotiation and sales contract that you don't completely understand.

3. Hire a competent local attorney to pave the way through local laws and customs.

4. Make use of American Chamber of Commerce offices located in many countries around the world.

5. Work closely with U.S. government agencies to learn of investment opportunities and political stumbling blocks.

6. Make the trip yourself to set up the business. Don't delegate.

7. Hire a local national to be general manager.

8. Carry reference letters from your home bank.

9. Apply for local government subsidies (they always exist).

10. In the beginning, do the marketing yourself.

11. Do enough market research in the beginning to be comfortable that you are making the right decision.

Global Markets for Contractors

The global scene is booming in the construction industry also. In practically every region of the world construction projects are being handled by large and small contractors from many different countries. Regardless of the construction niche you happen to be in, there is probably a bigger market for your specialty overseas than in America. Although major projects go to large prime contractors, the same way they do in the U.S., all these giants need and use small subcontractors to spread the risk.

Financing is easy. If the prime won't arrange it, several federal agencies stand ready to help.

To find out what projects are coming up, subscribe to any of several federal government publications or the *Journal of Commerce*. If bidding as a prime contractor is beyond your means, call on the major international engineering contractors such as Bechtel, Fluor, or Volker Stefens. Mergers have created fewer but larger contracting firms in Europe and an American subcontractor stands a good chance of getting in on the ground floor, especially if a project includes the installation of equipment.

As we all know, many Third World countries rely on money from the U.S government to build their infrastructures. Much of the aid flows through the Agency for International Development (USAID). A foreign government, and hence a prime contractor, stands a better chance of landing a USAID-funded contract if American-made equipment is used. And this gives an American subcontractor an entry as the broker-installer of goods shipped from American manufacturers.

Collecting from international customers can be a nightmare for small contractors taking on the role of prime contractor, especially if the customer is a foreign government. Unless the project is funded by USAID money, the foreign government has very little incentive to pay on schedule. On initial entry into global markets, your best bet is to tag along as a subcontractor to an international prime. Then insist on progress payments through LCs. At least progress payments allow you to stop work if a payment is missed, and no prime wants that to happen.

Recruiting competent supervisors is probably the biggest headache for smaller American contractors going global. Using

American project managers and supervisors hardly ever works, unless they have significant experience working overseas. On the other hand, several British employment agencies specialize in placing experienced, competent construction supervisors in the far corners of the globe. Check the *London Sunday Times* for advertisements in the "Help Wanted" section. Most weeks you will find at least half a dozen international construction personnel placement firms.

There are also a few reliable agencies in this country. Try the help wanted ads in the Sunday issue of the *New York Times, Miami Herald, Chicago Tribune,* or *Los Angeles Times,* depending on which part of the world the project is located.

International construction project supervisors are mobile. They move from project to project as the demand arises. Therefore, even though you have to hire them for one project, there is no need to keep them on the payroll after the projected ends. All payroll costs are built into the project bid price so hiring these project and technical supervisors won't add unrecoverable costs.

If you bid a project in an industrialized nation, there shouldn't be any problem hiring local laborers. In Third World countries this is frequently impossible. They just don't exist. The solution lies in importing labor from Pakistan, the Philippines, Mexico, or some other populated country. Labor brokers exist in all these countries. Just place your order and they manage all the details for locating the people and transporting them to the job site.

Just as with manufacturing, distribution, and service businesses, contractors must take on jobs during tough times they might not otherwise consider. Even if international projects don't appeal to you, rather than sitting around waiting for domestic markets to reopen, it's probably a good idea to give the global scene a chance. At least there are plenty of projects to go around. And you might be surprised. In spite of the difficulties with language, transportation, and cultural vagaries, most international construction jobs can be priced at significantly higher margins than domestic projects.

Advertising Overseas

Structuring an advertising campaign to test or open international markets can be a very costly effort. Large corporations have a hard enough time doing it. Small businesses usually find the cost prohibitive. Also, it's very difficult to control an advertising campaign in Argentina from Dallas or any other American location.

Most business owners find that relying on an EMC's sales representative network to handle the advertising and promotion programs in distant lands works best for exported products. If you are serious about opening a branch overseas, your best bet is to contract with one of the proficient foreign trading companies to get started in the market. The big, international trading companies are expensive. However, there are many smaller ones concentrating in specific countries or regions. When you choose your location, a quick visit to the local trade ministry can help locate several trading companies to choose from.

Tactics for Controlling Costs Overseas

Labor costs, material purchases, and facilities expenses must be incurred whether you manufacture in Boise or Bombay. Advertising, salespersons salaries or commissions and sales literature must be used whether selling to customers in Tucson or Tanzania. Telephones, electricity, and office equipment will be necessary whether located in New York or New Caledonia. The amount you pay for these costs varies with location but then so do the selling prices of your products or services. The same prudent controls exercised in this country to keep operating costs at a minimum apply universally, regardless of where or how products are made or distributed.

For most American companies, however, two types of expenses stand out as being significantly higher when doing business internationally: travel expenses and living expenses. These two costs must be controlled with vigor to reap the benefits of higher margins from foreign markets. If they are not tightly controlled, experience has shown that both travel and living expenses can and probably will become exorbitant.

International travel requires long, expensive plane trips. Airfares for U.S. international carriers as well as foreign airlines are substantially higher than those charged domestically. Fewer discounts are available. Less competition means fewer flights and airlines to choose from. Long, often overnight flights become extremely tiring and personnel require extra and costly amenities to recuperate once on the ground. Yet, large and small companies alike have found ways to keep travel expenses under control by establishing travel policies founded on five basic rules.

1. Everyone flies coach. No first or business class.

2. When flying from the U.S., always buy a round-trip ticket, leaving the return flight reservation open. Tickets usually cost less when purchased in the U.S.

3. Make flight reservations through a competent, internationally experienced travel agency. Since many overseas airlines and flight schedules are not listed in domestic computer systems, it takes an international agency to know how to do the job. They will pick the best airline and get the least expensive price.

4. Plan itineraries in a loop to avoid crisscrossing routes (e.g., New York to London to Rome to Cairo to Johannesburg to Rio to New York).

5. Make the trips as long as possible to reduce the amount of air travel. Avoid frequent short trips.

Overseas living expenses can also be kept down. For long stays, rent an apartment rather than a hotel room. It's much less expensive in the long run. When staying in hotels, choose those in the mid-range. No one makes money staying at Intercontinentals or Hiltons, except the hotel itself. On the other hand, a great many headaches can be avoided by staying out of the lowest priced hotels. In most parts of the world, bottom-of-the-ladder hotels are roach invested, fire-traps. Try for mid-priced hotels with cooking facilities. This saves the cost of at least one, maybe two meals per day. It's also a good idea to have the travel agent book the hotel reservation. An international travel agency knows which hotels are safe.

In some parts of the world, automobile transportation is necessary to get around the country. Stay away from Hertz, Avis, National, and other American companies. Local car rental firms are usually much less expensive. Better still, use local taxis rather than rental cars. In most parts of the world taxis cost much less than they do in the U.S. The general rule of thumb for experienced business travelers is to try to live the same way overseas they do when traveling at home. In most countries this will keep living costs to a minimum.

Conclusion

When your markets are shrinking something must be changed. New customers must be found, new markets opened, perhaps new products or services introduced. In tough times it's difficult to spend the money to make these moves. Therefore the time to begin analyzing the potential in your existing markets is before they begin to contract. At least then there might be time to cost effectively investigate and develop new markets or products.

The key in selective market penetration is to search out market niches that fit your abilities but that competition hasn't noticed or for some other reason hasn't entered. Being first in a new market niche can bring market control and margin maximization. It may not last forever, but in tough times market control for even a short time helps.

Advertising and promotion techniques to test and open new markets should be carefully controlled. Results may be not be known for several months. Meanwhile advertising dollars continue going out. Be certain that regardless of which media or approach you choose, the advertising program matches your new market objectives.

As the globalization of our economy grows in importance, new markets are opening overseas with burgeoning customer demand for virtually all products and services. When domestic markets shrink, smart business owners begin looking at applying selective market penetration techniques to these opportunities. Manufacturers, distributors, service companies, and contractors are already clamoring to enter global markets either through exporting or by establishing a presence overseas. More opportunities exist for small businesses than large, simply because there are more market niches that need filling. Large corporations tend to be more interested in developing large markets, leaving the niches to smaller companies.

The use of advertising techniques to test or open overseas markets can be a very expensive exercise. Most companies are better off using an EMC sales network or a foreign trading company to handle the market testing and initial sales promotions.

Chapter 12

A Worst Case Scenario
What to Do When All Else Fails

The wolves are at the door. All costs that won't ruin the business have been cut to the bone. Competition has voided all efforts to implement a protective marketing strategy. Assets have been sold, debt has been trimmed, and new market openings have been tried. Nothing works. Your business continues to slide. There is only one thing remaining to do. Take drastic action.

Many small businesses, unable to get control of their markets and with a bare-bones cost structure already in place, face the unhappy choice of closing the doors or making one last stab at surviving. This chapter includes ideas and recommendations for survival tactics that have worked for other business owners when times were very tough. Most of them have survived and gone on to more prosperous times. A few didn't make it.

By the time your business gets to the point of implementing these survival tactics, your market has probably deteriorated beyond repair. The only solution is to buy enough time to restructure your company, regroup your personnel, and find new markets or products.

Along with buying time to rebuild your business, it only makes sense to take measures to protect your personal assets. If the worst happens and you have to file for protection under the bankruptcy code, you certainly want to prevent a business creditor (bank or otherwise) from taking your house, car, investments, and other personal assets. Regardless of what happens to the business, protecting personal assets should be everyone's top priority.

Strategies to Protect Personal Assets

The very first step in devising a plan to protect your personal assets is to locate and retain a highly competent attorney who specializes in personal bankruptcy law. Not because you expect to file personal bankruptcy. No one does that until all other avenues are exhausted. You need a personal bankruptcy lawyer because personal bankruptcy laws are different in each state. They are state laws, not federal laws as in the case with corporate bankruptcy.

A competent (and I emphasize competent) personal bankruptcy lawyer can tell you exactly what actions will protect your assets in your state and the right time to take these actions to make them legal. The timing of the implementation of steps to protect personal assets is as important as the specific actions chosen.

There are two fool-proof ways to prevent losing personal assets to creditors, the IRS, or others with their hands out: keep your assets in a safe location where creditors and the rest of the vultures cannot reach them, or better yet, don't own any assets in your name.

Transfer Title to Personal Assets

If you don't own any assets no one can take them from you. With nothing to lose you can be much more aggressive when dealing with recalcitrant creditors. Also, with nothing to lose you don't have to worry about spending thousands of dollars on legal fees defending yourself in court actions.

To start with, if your business is not incorporated now, form a corporation quickly. A corporate shield won't provide absolute protection for business assets but it is certainly better than having title to these assets in your name. Corporations are easy and quick to form. You don't need an attorney.

Several companies in Delaware do nothing but form corporations for small businesses and then act as the legal representative. I've incorporated more than twenty businesses for myself and clients through The Company Corporation in Wilmington, Delaware. The cost is about $160 including all the paraphernalia needed to maintain a corporation plus about $60 a year in agent fees.

Once the corporation is formed, or if you already are incorporated, the next step is to put the title to your stock holdings in someone else's name. Transferring title to your spouse works well and avoids any complications from the IRS. Adult children whom you trust can also hold your shares. Other relatives can take title safely, assuming you trust them. A good friend agreed to take title to the shares in one of my companies that faced tough times.

Another possibility is to transfer your shares to a trust. Just be certain the trustee will vote the shares according to your instructions. To be absolutely safe, the trust must be irrevocable and you cannot be the trustee or the beneficiary. Does this mean you lose control of your business? Technically yes. But small business owners have been using this technique for years to protect their investment. As long as the trustee can be trusted, you shouldn't have any problem with the IRS or the courts and you can still direct the policies of your company.

Once steps are taken to protect business assets and your ownership interest it's time to turn to other assets you may own. Following is a partial list of personal assets that creditors, lawyers, and the IRS love to get their hands on

1. A residence—either a house or condo

2. Real estate investments—land, farms, vacation homes, rental property

3. Bank savings accounts

4. Bank investment instruments—certificates of deposit, money market accounts, and so on

5. Individual Retirement Accounts (IRAs) and other retirement or pension entitlements

6. Life insurance policies

7. Stock brokerage accounts

8. Investment stock and bond certificates

9. Limited partnership shares

10. U.S. savings bonds

11. Automobiles

12. Valuable collections—stamps, coins, antiques, jewelry

13. Valuable personal property—fur coats, diamond rings, paintings, sculptures, libraries, furniture

Nothing is safe as long as you own it. Granted, it's more difficult to lay claim to some of these assets than it is to others but if someone tries hard enough, everything you own can be lost.

In most states, any property held jointly with your spouse cannot be claimed in settlement of a lawsuit against you. But not necessarily. Take a residence, for example. In some states, creditors that win a settlement against you can claim your share of the house. Therefore, your spouse owns it along with outside creditors. When he or she sells it, the creditors take half the proceeds.

Joint bank accounts aren't foolproof either. Some creditor's lawyers go so far as to analyze the transactions in the account over the past three years and trace how many of the deposits came from you. If your deposits exceed 50 percent of the expenditures from the account, some courts allow plaintiffs to take that. They can also lay claim to 50 percent of any savings account or other investment held jointly with a spouse. So don't believe it when people tell you it's safe enough to keep everything in joint names. It doesn't work that way.

Another effective method is to set up a new corporation or series of corporations and spread the assets around. If you continue to hold controlling interest in each corporation you run the same risk as stated earlier. Nevertheless, the more complicated you can make it for anyone trying to seize your assets, the less likely they will persist.

Forming several corporations, each with varying ownership interests between you, your spouse, your children, relatives, and friends, some headquartered offshore, some domestic, tends to dissuade all but the most persistent of lawyers from dabbling in your affairs. And if they do try to break all the corporate shields they will find it to be a very costly process.

To be on the safe side, the best policy is the one I recommend to all my small business clients: transfer title to everything that you own of value to an outsider. Keep a small bank account for emergencies, but transfer everything else to your spouse, children, a trust, or relatives in the same way you did with for your company stock. Better to be safe than to be sorry.

Place Assets in Safekeeping

If you don't want to transfer title to assets, or you don't know of anyone you can trust to hold these assets for your use and benefit, then the only other alternative is to place as many assets as possible in safekeeping. No, this does not mean a safe deposit box. Bank safe deposit boxes can be opened by outsiders for any number of reasons. That is not the place to put valuables you want to keep away from creditors.

A much better alternative, although somewhat convoluted, is to assign all your valuables to a trust, just like the earlier recommendation for your company shares. As long as the trust is irrevocable and you are not either the trustee or the beneficiary, the trust shield is difficult to break.

As an added precaution, you can set up this trust offshore in a private, protected, riskfree bank. Although the IRS and the Department of Justice have penetrated the bank security of many so-called tax haven countries, a few still remain as safe havens for assets. Assuming, of course, that the assets were not obtained through illegal means. Even the staunchest tax haven countries have agreements with the U.S. government to break the privacy shield for drug-related or other criminally acquired assets.

I have stopped recommending Switzerland as a safe haven. Swiss banks have succumbed too often to both U.S. and other pressures to break the privacy shield and are therefore no longer trustworthy. The same is true for Bermuda, the Bahamas, the Netherland Antilles, Luxembourg, and several other countries used as safe havens in the past. I can however recommend Liechtenstein and the Cayman Islands as continuing secure locations. Most Americans prefer Grand Cayman because of its close proximity.

Nearly every Fortune 500 company has a bank account in Grand Cayman. Wealthy private individuals continue to flock to the island to open accounts and transfer assets. I have helped several clients set up trusts in Grand Cayman. Recently, small business owners are beginning to realize the advantages of protecting their assets in this manner. Needless to say, the trust business is booming on the island. By the way, Grand Cayman has no taxes whatsoever, so any income your assets earn while in the trust is taxfree. When you repatriate the cash back to the U.S., these earnings are taxed at normal rates.

Those are the two best ways to protect your assets from nefarious creditors: transfer title to other individuals or corporations, or move your assets to an offshore safe haven. I urge you to consider either or both alternatives early enough to avoid legal timing difficulties. The more complicated and costly you make it for creditors to locate and seize your assets, the less likely they will even try. Surprisingly, even the IRS has limits beyond which it will not continue the chase. Even in good times, asset protection makes prudent sense. In tough times it is imperative for financial security and, more important, for peace of mind.

Once assets are firmly under lock and key you can proceed to aggressive tactics to save your business. The first step is to determine just how much cash-flow you have and how to apportion it to various creditors.

Budget Cash

Operating budgets were described in chapter 2 as a means of controlling a cost-reduction plan. Under a worst case scenario, after you have tried all the cost-reductions you can think of, it's time to use budgets for a different purpose: to allocate available cash to hungry creditors and to be sure there is still have enough left over to run the business. This requires knowing exactly how much cash is on hand every day, and how much can be expected to come in each week. Such small increments are essential to maximize the use of what you have. The smaller the increment, the tighter the control, and the easier it is to allocate cash to the most important creditors first.

By following the cash-flow plan described in chapter 1, you should have a pretty good idea of how much will be coming in this week and next week. Beyond that, contingencies, fluctuating sales, and a variety of other unforeseen events continually change the forecast. But for two weeks it should be reasonably accurate.

I like to use a 7-column accounting pad. Others prefer the back of an an envelop. It doesn't make any difference what you use. Just record on paper how much cash you have on hand right now and how much you expect to come in this week. Subtract the weekly gross payroll (and payroll taxes) and building rent (if it's due). The balance tells you how much you can afford to pay against all the bills you owe and how much you can draw for yourself.

One brief comment about payroll. Be sure to subtract the *gross* payroll, not the amount of the payroll checks. The difference represents withholdings from employees, and that money belongs to them. Legally, you can get by without paying almost everyone and still survive for a while. That is not true for withheld payroll taxes. Whether your business is incorporated or not, you can be personally fined and jailed by the IRS for not paying payroll taxes. It's silly to take that risk.

It's almost as important to pay the rent. The last thing you need at this stage is to be thrown out by the building owner.

Paying interest and principal on loans to banks is also crucial. However, if you follow the tips from chapter 9 about restructuring debt payments you should have some relief here already. Also, bear in mind that it takes a bank a long time to enter into a foreclosure action—usually six months or more. Asset-based lenders are different. But even with ABLs, a borrower normally has at least three or four months before the axe falls.

Once you know how much cash remains after payroll and rent, the next step is to determine what bills to pay. Now it's time to put together a schedule of supplier invoices, past due taxes, utility bills, professional fees, employee expense accounts, and any other invoices or statements already received.

Tactics for Scheduling Supplier Payments

The purpose of going through all the machinations of cash budgeting and allocating cash payments is to be certain that you don't run out of cash to operate the business. Obviously, if there was more cash coming in than going out there would be no reason to perform this exercise. But when the reverse occurs, when a company owes more money to creditors than it receives from customers, something must give. And in survival planning the underlying assumption is that creditors have more flexibility to withstand cash shocks than you do. Therefore creditors must help bail you out by extending additional credit.

To add some order to this chaos, I have found it very helpful to begin by listing all bills on hand regardless of source, and then lay them out according to how old they are: in other words an aged listing of accounts payable. The bigger the company, the more invoices to handle, and it can become very confusing trying to keep track of what has been paid to whom without some type of listing updated each week.

I also find it helpful at this stage to anticipate as close as possible how much cash will be coming in and what new bills will be coming in each week for the next four weeks. When you talk to creditors you then have some idea when you might be able to pay them.

The third listing that can be very helpful is a schedule of amounts that will be payable each week for four weeks out in priority sequence. For example, you know that bills for electricity, telephone, rent, gross payroll, fuel, and so on, are payments that must be made on a regular, recurring basis or the business will cease to function. These critical, recurring bills are at the top of the list. They are paid first.

Utility and telephone bills all have a billing date listed on the invoice. You can make a one-time cash saving by not paying the bills the first month and then always paying one month in arrears from then on. As long as the utility receives payment before the third-month billing goes out (you can tell from the billing dates on the invoices) you're safe. This give you an extra thirty days to pay the first bill.

If you can find out when your landlord hits the hot button you can play the same game with rent and make a one-time savings of thirty days. The same approach can be used for credit card balances. With credit cards however, the date you finally pay must coincide with each bank's instructions to avoid interest expense.

Once the regular bills are taken care of, you can begin scheduling the normal supplier invoices. Obviously, you can stretch some further than others. Regular suppliers will usually grant you sixty days, maybe longer. Invoices from infrequent purchases can be stretched a lot further without permanent damage—some as long as six months. The idea is to pay only those bills you have to in order to keep the business going and avoid COD deliveries, if at all possible.

Eventually, if conditions really get tough, you will probably have to negotiate with suppliers for extended terms. Following are a few tips for delaying supplier payments or negotiating long-term payments.

Tips for Negotiating with Creditors

When push comes to shove suppliers of materials, supplies, and purchased services always get paid last, after bank payments, payroll, recurring bills, and taxes. This back-door approach to getting additional credit won't win any friends in your creditors' ranks but there usually is no other choice.

The first reaction from creditors when told their payment on account has been delayed is to cut you off from further product deliveries or services until old invoices are paid. You obviously can't let this happen if you need those materials or services to keep the business running. The rest can wait, but negotiations with critical suppliers should begin immediately. Larger suppliers will probably negotiate a payment schedule—you pay so much each week or each month until the old invoices are liquidated. Try to negotiate new purchases on forty-five- to sixty-day terms. This may not work, but if you adhere to your scheduled payments of old invoices, it might. At least get thirty-day terms. COD deliveries are deadly and only exacerbate the cash problem.

Suppliers are similar to banks. Most recognize that it is in their best interest to keep your company going so you will purchase more of their products or services. Few operating companies opt for foreclosure because they know that recovery will probably be less than the amount owed. Also they will then lose a customer, which might hurt over the long run even more than not getting paid for old invoices.

Next in line behind critical suppliers come those small companies that will be in as bad shape as your company if you don't pay. Small repair shops, your independent bookkeeper, the service station where you buy gas for your car, the independent grocery, pharmacy, and other retail establishments, the local newspaper, small subcontractors (if you have a publishing business, please include your authors), and so on.

These are small businesses just like yours. You have to live with their owners every day. When times improve, you will be good business partners once again. Taking care of these suppliers as soon as possible not only makes living in a community easier and more pleasant, it helps your public image as a caring business owner. And that can pay big dividends later on.

Suppliers of employee benefits deserve to get paid next: group insurance carriers, automobile fleet insurance companies, state unemployment and worker's compensation funds, your share of federal social security payments, and other employee related expenses. In passing, it should be noted that you can't go to jail for not paying state payroll taxes or your share of FICA. But you can end up behind bars for reneging on taxes withheld from employees' pay checks.

Federal and state estimated income taxes, sales and use taxes, property taxes, legal, accounting, and other professional fees, noncritical large suppliers, and nonessential outside contractors (e.g., janitorial service, equipment maintenance contracts, equipment leases, and so on), round out the list. Chances are, however, that if you have enough money to pay these creditors you won't have to go through this exercise at all.

The following priority list is one I have consistently used with clients. It affords a quick reference for scheduling the payment of old bills and selecting which vendors rate the greatest negotiating effort.

1. Payroll and employee withholding taxes

2. Building/office rent

3. Utility and telephone

4. Interest on bank loans (see chapter 9)

5. Principal on bank loans (see chapter 9)

6. Purchases of materials and services crucial to keeping the business going

7. Small service and retail businesses, usually local

8. Employee benefits, including state payroll taxes and employer's share of FICA taxes

9. Federal and state income and other taxes

10. Noncritical purchases and services

How to Leverage Better Payment Terms

It is remarkable how agreeable creditors can be to stretching out payments when you have a bargaining chip. As in any negotiation, the party with the most to lose or the most to gain is always on the defensive. Other than meeting payroll, there are only two conditions that might create circumstances more detrimental to you than to the creditor: being evicted from the building that houses your business or not receiving critical materials and services to keep the business going.

There isn't a great deal that can be done about this. You have to house your business and you must have materials and services to make and sell products. That's why landlords and critical suppliers are at the top of the payment priority list.

You can get some leverage though. Most lessors would rather work out an arrangement with you than go to the expense and aggravation of a formal eviction. In tough times, occupancy rates for commercial and industrial real estate nearly always plummet. It becomes a renter's market. That being the case, you can probably work out a deferral of rent for at least several months. That should give you some breathing space.

You might have to acquiesce to higher monthly payments over the balance of the lease period but in a crisis situation, it might be worth it. You also might be able to negotiate the same rental and merely add the deferred period on to the end of the lease. A six-month rent deferral is not uncommon, and many lessees get much more.

Critical suppliers can be more difficult, but not always. Except in very unusual cases, given a little time and effort you should be able to come up with competitive suppliers for materials and services. It can't hurt to try negotiating extended payment terms using the threat of turning your on-going orders over to a competitor.

In most cases, when negotiating for extended payment terms, a creditor has more to lose (what you owe the creditor or legal costs to bring suit) or gain (future sales) than you do. At least try to make creditors think that's the case.

Assuming you have taken reasonable precautions to safeguard your personal assets as described earlier in this chapter, including your ownership of the business, the worst thing that can happen is to be forced to liquidate your business. Granted, this can be a blow to the ego, and it might cut off your source of income for a while, but resiliency usually wins out and you can recover.

As long as creditors believe that you have less to lose than they do, you remain in the driver's seat when negotiating. The ultimate threat a creditor can throw out is to force you into bankruptcy. If you make it clear that this won't hurt and you have other plans for the future anyway, a creditor's leverage disappears in the wind.

Leveraging through the Bankruptcy Code

Conversely, you can use the threat of filing bankruptcy to get almost anything you want from creditors. Unsecured creditors know that once a company has filed a Chapter 11 bankruptcy one or both of two situations will happen: the creditor will eventually receive at best a small percentage of what is due (5 or 10 cents on the dollar), or the creditor will have to wait for an extended period before receiving any payment (usually several years). If a creditor doesn't understand this it won't take long to lay out the ground rules.

Several tactics can be deployed from this leverage. Before getting into specific suggestions, however, a brief explanation of the Bankruptcy Code is in order.

Types of Bankruptcies

There are four types of bankruptcies applicable to most small businesses and business owners.

1. Chapter 7—Liquidation Bankruptcy

   A Chapter 7 filing can be initiated by the business owner or by creditors. The purpose in this form is to liquidate assets at auction or otherwise and divide the proceeds between creditors. It is usually completed within ninety days of filing.

2. Chapter 11—Reorganization Bankruptcy

   A Chapter 11 filing means that the creditors of a company cannot take any action to force payment of debts while the company works out a court approved plan of reorganization. The owner continues to operate the company while the reorganization plan is worked out. This plan normally results in unsecured creditors getting a fraction of what is owed them and releasing all further claims.

3. Chapter 12—Family-Farmer Bankruptcy

Chapter 12 is a relatively new feature of the Code and applies only to a family-owned business with at least 50 percent of its income from agriculture and debts under $1.5 million.

4. Chapter 13—Wage Earner Bankruptcy

Chapter 13 is designed for individuals with a steady source of income and total debt of less than $450,000, of which the unsecured portion cannot be more than $100,000.

The Risks of a Chapter 11 Filing

Even though a Chapter 11 filing can be an effective way to force a restructuring of bank debt and to reduce the amounts owed creditors, all kinds of difficult problems arise. If you are considering such an action be aware of two legal points unique to bankruptcy law. The fundamental principle under bankruptcy law is that an individual is presumed guilty until proven innocent: just the reverse of other laws. It is the court's duty, under law, to protect and save the company—not the business owner—which leads to the second point.

Second, a company protected by Chapter 11, prodded by creditors and the trustee, has the right (it's really an obligation) to recover "preferential payments" from insiders. If the debtor is a corporation, an insider is defined as any director or officer of the corporation or any person that has control of the corporation.

Preferential payments are any payments made to an insider while the corporation is insolvent (liabilities exceed assets) for up to twelve months prior to filing. By definition, the company is considered insolvent for ninety days prior to filing. Any payments for any reason made to an insider during the twelve-month period prior to filing (assuming the company is insolvent during this period) or any payments made in the ninety days preceding filing must be paid back to the company. Salaries, bonuses, dividends, travel expense reimbursements, insurance premium payments, pension plan contributions, and any other payments made by the company to, or on behalf of the insider are included.

As an insider you cannot win. You have no right to these payments and must return them, even though you own the company. That's how an individual is presumed guilty under the bankruptcy laws. So think twice before electing a Chapter 11. You could end up much worse than you were before.

Gain Advantage with Threat of Bankruptcy

Obviously, filing bankruptcy is a last resort. Fortunately, you may never need to file but you can use the threat of doing so to exact concessions from creditors. This game gets nasty, but when you are sinking, nearly anything is better than going under.

Threatening to take the company into bankruptcy works especially well with suppliers that have sold material or services to your company for many years. It also works effectively if your purchases have been sizable relative to a supplier's other customers. In either case the supplier should be further ahead by keeping you as a customer than by forcing you into bankruptcy. If they really believe you'll take the company to the ropes, most are willing to negotiate a long-term payment schedule and other arrangements to help you over a cash crunch.

Another effective tactic using the threat of filing bankruptcy is to offer to settle an old bill at a fraction of what is owed. Knowing it will probably have to settle for 5 or 10 cents on the dollar by agreeing to a bankruptcy reorganization plan and recognizing the effort and time involved in informing and meeting with creditor's committees and bankruptcy attorneys, many suppliers gladly take 30, 40, or 50 cents on the dollar to keep you out of the courts.

By retaining a continuing business relationship, regular suppliers can probably recoup any current losses through additional business or higher prices later on. Once you are in bankruptcy, the game is over.

Another effective tactic is to agree to take future deliveries of materials on consignment and pay for them only when they are sold. Although a supplier must wait for payment, at least a sale is made and payment will come eventually. Certainly better than seeing you fold.

The threat of filing a Chapter 11 can also be effective leverage when dealing with employee groups or collective bargaining units. Many small business owners have been able to exact unsecured term loans from unions to keep the company alive. From the employees' point of view, almost anything is better than going into bankruptcy with the possibility of losing their jobs.

I should be quick to point out, however, that the threat of filing under Chapter 11 provisions won't get you much from state or federal agencies to whom you owe money. The IRS, state unemployment funds, environmental protection agencies, or other governmental bureaucracies have no interest in seeing your business survive. Politicians pay lip service to saving jobs, but I have never seen a governmental agency willing to reduce an obligation to make it happen. Of course, giant corporations such as Chrysler, Lockheed, or Continental Bank, are a different story.

Banks are also tough to negotiate with. As secured creditors, banks know they have top priority in a Chapter 11 filing. They also know that assuming their collateral value is at least equal to the outstanding loan balance, if push comes to shove they will recoup their money through a liquidation. On the other hand, with the exception of asset-based lenders, most banks have no internal mechanism to handle or monitor a liquidation. And therein lies additional bargaining leverage.

Tactics for Negotiating Debt Reduction after Filing Chapter 11
If you actually do file for protection under Chapter 11, a different type of negotiating leverage occurs. Now, your negotiating strength lies in the threat to take the company into a Chapter 7 liquidation when hardly anyone wins. This becomes especially valuable leverage when negotiating with banks and other secured creditors.

As secured lenders, banks retain the highest position in the priority of creditors under the Bankruptcy Code. They have the least to lose if you do file under Chapter 11. They know that if there is any chance at all of reorganizing and coming out of bankruptcy, they will get paid in full.

A Chapter 7 liquidation, however, is a different matter entirely. A liquidation sale of equipment, machinery, vehicles, or inventory, seldom, if ever, produces cash even close to the amount of the secured loan. And all lenders know this. Therefore, once in Chapter 11, business owners have a significant amount of leverage in dealing with lenders and other secured creditors simply by threatening to liquidate the company.

It doesn't take much negotiating to parlay this leverage into a renegotiated loan agreement. If you get to this point, a few of the terms you might want to consider when rewriting the loan document are an extension of the due date, a moratorium on principal payments, a moratorium on both interest and principal payments for several months or years, and a conversion of short-term loans to long-term debt. In some cases, business owners have been able to trade some of the debt to lenders for an equity share in the company.

Trading Equity for Debt

Trading equity for debt works with unsecured creditors as well as banks. Chapter 9 pointed out how giving up a share of the company in exchange for cash to pay down bank loans works effectively for restructuring debt loads. The same tactic can be employed to satisfy nonbank creditors.

The size of your company or the business you are in doesn't make much difference in this case. If you are willing to give up a share of future profits in exchange for debt forgiveness now, an equity/debt swap might be one answer to staying alive. Some suppliers seem to be more amenable to this tactic than others.

Large suppliers are generally more willing to extending payment terms or even reducing the amounts you owe for quicker payment. Small suppliers, however, at least those who are themselves facing the brink, frequently see an opportunity to influence your decision to continue buying from them. As opposed to actually laying out cash to help you, as described in chapter 9, this time around they get a share in your company without any additional cost to them (other than not getting paid what they are owed, of course).

Employees react even better to an equity share in exchange for back pay or in exchange for foregoing future vacations, raises, or benefits. When pushing the panic button, small businesses can ill afford employee vacations. If you didn't need the employee to do the work he or she would have been included in your cost reduction program. If you could afford additional employee benefits you sure wouldn't be looking at negotiating deals with suppliers and banks. A small share of the company is often enough incentive for employees to agree to stop retirement plan contributions and other cash expenditures on their behalf.

Finally, although lawyers, consultants, auditors, and other professionals or outside contractors to whom you owe money will probably not be interested in foregoing their receivable for an equity share, it can't hurt to ask. You could do a lot worse than sharing ownership with a qualified management consultant.

Other Tactics When the Chips Are Down

Here are a few other tips you might consider as last resort measures. They might not be very palatable, but business owners have used them effectively to get out of cash binds.

Borrow on personal credit cards. With credit card companies eager to attract new customers, lines of credit totaling $5,000, $10,000 or more are not uncommon. Try coercing your credit card company into higher limits. Then use credit cards to purchase materials and services rather than buying on open account. When the bill comes in you have thirty days to pay without interest. If you are willing to pay exorbitant interest, you can virtually take years to pay off the balance, and continue to charge new purchases. This amounts to an additional open line of credit—albeit at a very high interest rate.

Borrow from the IRS. Do not use employee withholding taxes for anything. As pointed out earlier, this can land you in jail. But you can borrow from the IRS by not paying estimated income taxes and even by not sending a check along with your annual return. Of course, interest and penalties will be attached, and eventually you'll have to pay up, but in the meantime you can use the cash you have to run the business. It always takes time for the IRS to catch up. Being able to use your cash for six months to a year might help get over the cash crunch.

Bring in a partner. For many entrepreneurs this idea violates everything they believe in. The mere thought of sharing ownership with a partner turns them off. Nevertheless, as a last resort, partners can bring in cash. This might be the time to consider a partner. Assuming, or course, you can find one who is interested and has cash.

Take out personal loans. Many small business owners consider this alternative right in the beginning as soon as cash gets tight. Although it might be a solution in some instances, it is a dangerous step. As the earlier part of this chapter described, the one thing you should do for long-term survival (and peace of mind) is to protect personal assets. As soon as you borrow money for the business against these assets, they are no longer protected. If the business eventually fails you could lose everything, not just the business. Yet, time and again, personal loans are used to fund businesses.

If you own a house and have a fair amount of equity built up in it, a home equity loan is one of the easiest types to arrange. Just remember that in tough times personal mortgage payments can be just as difficult to meet as business debt service payments.

Although recession-proofing your personal income and investment is beyond the scope of this book, as a small business owner you should really consider the two inseparable. Bankruptcy laws apply to individuals as well as businesses and its bad enough to have your business go on the rocks without suffering the same fate in your personal life. Although a mortgage loan on your home—either a first or second mortgage—is certainly a way to raise additional cash, think twice before going this route.

Most of us, if pressed to the wall, can probably come up with other sources for borrowing personal funds. Perhaps another loan on your car. Or borrowing against personal savings and investment accounts. IRAs and Keogh plan accounts can serve as collateral. Stamp and coin collections, antiques, paintings, and so on can also secure personal loans. All those assets we talked about earlier that you should protect from creditors can be pledged to secure additional borrowings. But beware of the risk.

In closing, and as a last ditch effort to try to persuade you not you use personal assets to raise business cash, the case of Joseph Klein, hotelier, developer, and rabid entrepreneur serves as an excellent example of Murphy's Law.

> Joe built and owned five hotels. Over the years he made a substantial fortune speculating on land, and on building and selling hotels. Enjoying the lavish lifestyle, Joe invested heavily in antiques, paintings, other works of art, expensive sports cars, and stretch limousines, as well as a personal residence valued at well over $2 million.
>
> As the financial markets collapsed, Joe found it increasingly difficult to raise construction loans. Cost overruns on his last four projects resulted in defaults on several loans. Pressed by creditors and banks alike, Joe began borrowing against his wealth of personal assets. He also acquiesced to several personal guarantees against both business and personal loans.
>
> As the recession deepened, room occupancy fell off dramatically and the cash-flow Joe had counted on to meet the variety of debt service payments he had committed to didn't materialize. Pushed to the wall, Joe considered filing bankruptcy on his properties but his attorney warned him that all the property loans and personal loans were cross-collateralized along with his personal guarantees. If the business collapsed, so would Joe personally. Eventually creditors forced a Chapter 7 against one of the hotels. The house of cards collapsed. In less than six months, Joe lost everything: his hotels, his house, and all his personal treasures.

No magic formula raises the yoke of recessionary pressures. No consultant, loan officer, government agency, financial guru, or author can make the hurt of tough times go away. When all is said and done, business owners must solve their own problems in the best way they know how. It has always been thus, and probably always will be.

We all know the risks of entrepreneurship. We also know the rewards, both monetary and otherwise, from resolving our own dilemmas in our own ways.

The secret to recession-proofing a business in any industry of any size is to implement the same cost controls and protective marketing strategies discussed throughout this book well in advance of economic and market pressures. Companies that practice prudent cash management and careful planning of production, selling, and administrative activities as a standard operating procedure always come through tough times in the best shape. When your business begins declining the job becomes much harder. The time to act is now, before the fireball hits.